Early Deprivation
of Empathic Care

Published under the Auspices
of the Waters Foundation
Framingham, Massachusetts

Early Deprivation of Empathic Care

by

John Leopold Weil, M.D.

Judge Baker Children's Center
Harvard Medical School

INTERNATIONAL UNIVERSITIES PRESS
Madison   Connecticut

Library of Congress Cataloging-in-Publication Data

Weil, John Leopold, 1920–
    Early deprivation of empathic care / by John Leopold Weil.
      p. cm.
    Includes bibliographical references and indexes.
    ISBN 0-8236-1525-1
    1. Emotional deprivation. 2. Empathy. I. Title.
    [DNLM: 1. Infant Psychology. 2. Parent-Child Relations.
    3. Psychosocial Deprivation—in infancy & childhood. WS 105.5.D3
    W422e]
    RJ507.E56W45   1992
    155.4'1241—dc20
    DNLM/DLC
    for Library of Congress   91-30988
                                      CIP

Dedicated to
Professor Leonard Solomon
with Gratitude for his Inestimable Help

Table of Contents

Acknowledgments

This is the time to thank each of the wise and helpful friends who have contributed to all aspects of this manuscript.

First, I want to thank Professor Leonard Solomon to whom this book is dedicated. From the beginning, with kindness and patience, Dr. Solomon would direct me to pertinent information. This wise man also listened, supported, corrected, and elaborated upon my efforts.

Next I want to thank Dr. Richard Waters for his devoted and insightful editing and for his extended help in reorganizing *Early Deprivation*. It is thanks to his skill that the text's presentation became effectively integrated.

Equally important has been the help extended by Linda Haines and Cherie Potts. Linda Haines spent many hours each week in the process of checking, editing, and correcting the gradually emerging text. At the same time she succeeded in breathing life into this work. So did Cherie Potts contribute to the book's development as she prepared the ever-changing manuscript with the help of her complex word-processing facilities. She personally dedicated her capabilities to the advancement of this manuscript and royally delivered her work with thoughtfulness and kindness.

Another contributor to the text is Robin Esterberg, who translated journal articles from the original German. Robin's capabilities, her interest, and enthusiasm made the task of translation a pleasure.

Dr. Dale Moyer reviewed *Early Deprivation* not only early in its development but also in its final phases. Dr. Moyer's positive final review was coupled with constructive suggestions pertaining to current references. I am deeply grateful for his interest in my endeavors. So am I indebted to Evelyn Goldsmith, Susan Garland, Ann Haggerty, and my wife, Geraldine Rickard Weil, for their devoted support, and to Thomas Todd and Norman Comeau of Thomas Todd Printers in Boston for their dedicated work in creating the artistic figures and tables upon which this text presentation depends. Likewise, I am grateful to Jackie Cannon of International Universities Press, for her caring expertise in preparing this book.

Acknowledgments are extended to the University of Queensland Press, Queensland, Australia, 4067, for their permission granted to quote herein passages from *Psychological Deprivation in Childhood*, 1975, by J. Langmeier and L. Matejcek.

Finally, my closing thoughts turn to the Waters Foundation of Framingham, Massachusetts, and to International Universities Press. I want to thank not only the members of the Waters Foundation, Mr. and Mrs. James Waters and Dr. Richard Waters, but also Dr. Margaret Emery, Editor-in-Chief, and Martin Azarian, President, of International Universities Press for their faith in my efforts to help children.

Introduction

During the past fifty years, much has been written about symptoms associated with emotional deprivation among infants. Specialists from the fields of pediatrics, psychoanalysis, clinical psychology, animal psychology, and neuropharmacology, have contributed step by step to the understanding of this important field of investigation. Today, the individual pieces of information contributed from these numerous disciplines seem ready to be fitted together to form a dynamic picture of emerging symptoms. The purpose of this monograph is to shed light upon such connections between early deprivation of empathic care and the emergence of complex emotional symptoms during infancy, early childhood, and adolescence.

This monograph focuses upon the emotional effects of deprivation of empathic care during infancy in relation to two basic axes of behavior: (1) an axis describing the degrees of arousal, that is, involving hyper- and hypo-states of arousal, and (2) an axis describing degrees of pleasure–displeasure (Emde, Kligman, Reich, and Wade, 1978, pp. 134–136, 142; Emde, 1983, pp. 180–181). The psychological importance of these two axes is reflected in the observation that the vicissitudes of the arousal axis involve feelings of *being alive*, the infant's "highs and lows" based upon the degree to which consciousness and wakefulness are aroused (Lindsley, 1952, p. 445), whereas the vicissitudes of the pleasure–displeasure axis involve the degree to which living is or is not rewarded and the degree to which living involves positive or negative reactions to ongoing contacts (Olds, 1958, pp. 246–248; Olds, 1964, pp. 26, 32; Heath, 1964, pp. 224–229, 235; Heath and Gallant, 1964, pp. 87, 90, 96; Bishop, Elder, and Heath, 1964, p. 70; Emde, 1984, p. 40). The importance of the reactions associated with the pleasure–displeasure axis is also suggested by the observation that a dearth of supply lines of pleasure below a given homeostatic level among deprived infants is regularly followed by an increased incidence of sickness and death. This conclusion is in keeping with Spitz's observations (1945, pp. 59, 70; 1946, pp. 115–116).

In particular, this monograph deals with the emergence of compensatory supply lines of pleasure in behalf of restoring life-essential, stable homeostatic states of pleasure among infants who have been chronically deprived of empathic care.

In brief, the areas of investigation considered in each chapter of this monograph as outlined in the Table of Contents refer to early deprivation of empathic care as an antecedent for: pathology occurring during infancy, childhood, and adolescence associated with (1) *HYPER* and *HYPO States* of arousal; (2) chronic losses of pleasure; and (3) compensatory supply lines of pleasure. Findings pertaining to these symptomatic reactions taking place among infants deprived of empathic care are covered in chapters 1 through 5. Findings pertaining to such symptomatic reactions among adolescents who as infants had been deprived of empathic care are covered in chapters 6 through 8.

Such a focus upon the long-term symptomatic effects of

early emotional deprivation has been of particular interest during this past decade at a time when investigators are concluding that extreme deprivation during infancy constitutes one of the most serious forms of child abuse. This concept was directly summarized by a headline of the *New York Times*, December 20, 1983, which read "Emotional Deprivation Seen as Devastating Form of Child Abuse" (Brody, 1983, p. C1). However, such headlines should not obscure a realization that deprivation of empathic care among infants can be described along a continuum ranging from "common practice" to "child abuse," much as physical punitive stimulation of children can be measured along such a continuum describing the magnitude of punitive stimulation. For this reason, this monograph will focus upon symptom formation in relation to mild as well as severe deprivation of empathic care during infancy.

CHAPTER 1

Deprivation During Infancy, a Source for Psychological and Physical Deterioration

HISTORICAL PERSPECTIVES

Initial Reports Pertaining to Infant Deprivation[1]

By 1540 when the case of a three-year-old Hessian boy raised by wild animals was first described, there appeared a cursory interest in children who had been severely deprived during infancy. In 1767, Linnaeus was able to report ten cases of children raised by wild animals (1758, p. 20; cited by Zingg, 1940, p. 488, and by Langmeier and Matejcek, 1975, p. 35). By 1940, Zingg reported, in all, thirty-one relatively well-authen-

---

[1] Many of the historical findings presented in this chapter were collected, organized, and summarized by two Czechoslovakian investigators, J. Langmeier and Z. Matejcek, at the Postgraduate Medical Institute in Prague. Their bibliography of over 1000 pertinent references to clinical studies and research carried out in the Western and Eastern European countries and in the United States provides a wealth of material which otherwise would be difficult to recover (Langmeier and Matejcek, 1975, pp. 417–481).

1

ticated cases of children raised in isolation in the home or in the wild. Among these children are "the Wild Boy of Aveyron" raised in the wild at the end of the eighteenth century, Kasper Hauser, who was recovered from a dark cellar in Nuremberg in 1829, and the "Wolf Children," Amala and Kamala, who were found far from civilization in India in 1920 (Zingg, 1940, pp. 495–504; cited by Langmeier and Matejcek, 1975, pp. 36, 38, 40).

Langmeier and Matejcek also reviewed more recent case histories of eight isolated children including two of their own cases. Thereupon they summarized the overall findings reported from such studies involving total human isolation.

> Although reports on children who are partially or completely socially isolated are less accurate than we might wish, they afford a number of tentative conclusions. Social isolation is clearly the most deprivational situation. Its results are very marked. The mental development of the child is grossly retarded, speech is not developed at all, useful social habits are not established. The child appears to be severely feeble-minded and is often regarded as such [Langmeier and Matejcek, 1975, p. 44].

> Even in cases where improvement occurs in intellectual development, however, serious personality disorders remain. These children are at first fearful of people; later relationships are unstable, undifferentiated, strikingly obsequious, and reflect an insatiable demand for love and attention. Sexual behavior is either autoerotic or uncontrolled and undiscriminating. Emotional behavior is ... characterized by a hunger for intense stimulation ... and by a very low frustration tolerance [Langmeier and Matejcek, 1975, pp. 44–45].

The Emergence of Societal Concern for Deprived Infants

Serious investigation of deprivation among infants was not set in motion until the beginning of the twentieth century. At that time, an awareness of the devastating effects of deprivation among infants gradually emerged in connection with the placement of orphaned infants within large impersonal institutions where numbers of the infants became sick and died. One of the major foundling homes in Germany had a mortality rate of 71.5 percent for infants in the first year of life (Schlossmann, 1920, p. 1318; Eckstein-Schlossmann, 1926, p. 31); and among ten asylums in the United States death rates of infants admitted during the first year of life varied from 31.7 percent to 75 percent by the end of the second year (Chapin, 1915, p. 725). Such infants were described as suffering from "atrophia infantum," "debilitas vitae," and "marasmus" (Langmeier and Matejcek, 1975, p. 72).

Attention was first drawn to the medical sources for the infants' deterioration. During the period 1912 to 1920, A. Schlossmann, an outstanding German pediatrician, found he could decrease the mortality rate of institutionalized infants from 71.5 percent to 17.3 percent by providing quarantined protective care to combat the spread of infection. To accomplish this purpose, he placed infants in cubicles where they could be protected from germs; they also were vaccinated, provided with aseptic medical care, and fed balanced nutritional diets (Schlossmann, 1920, p. 1319; 1923, pp. 189–192, 195, 197; Eckstein–Schlossmann, 1926, p. 31; for a bibliography, see Langmeier and Matejcek, 1975, pp. 72–73).

Despite such medical precautions, however, large numbers of institutionalized infants continued to deteriorate and to die (Eckstein-Schlossmann, 1926, pp. 32, 36, 38). By 1925, another renowned German pediatrician, M. Pfaundler, reached the conclusion that "hospitalism," a syndrome involving developmental disturbances accompanied by physical and mental deterioration, arose from mass care: a lack of personal, maternal care among institutionalized infants (Pfaundler, 1925, pp. 3, 4, 13–17; Langmeier and Matejcek, 1975, p. 73). Thereupon, there arose a controversy as to whether pathological deterioration among infants could best be limited by improving medical care within foundling institutions as recommended by Schlossmann, or by eliminating impersonal institutional care altogether and returning infants to their own mothers or foster mothers as recommended by Pfaundler.

Controlled Psychological Studies of Emotional Deprivation in Infancy as a Source for "Hospitalism"

Gradually, an increasing accumulation of evidence directed attention to the conclusion that more than medical precautions were needed if foundlings were to be protected from physical and mental deterioration. An exemplary baby institute, established by Schlossmann to prove the beneficial effects of medical attention and sanitary care of institutionalized infants, failed to put an end to hospitalism, and even Schlossmann's close colleague and daughter reported that institutional children did not develop as well as children growing up in a family setting (Eckstein-Schlossmann, 1926, p. 38).

The Vienna school of psychologists under the direction of Charlotte Buhler thereupon began a systematic investigation of emotional causes for hospitalism and in this way launched a truly psychological investigation of early deprivation (Langmeier and Matejcek, 1975, p. 73). To carry out these investigations, it was first necessary for the Vienna psychologists to devise objective tests to measure infants' mental, emotional, and social development. To this end, in 1928 Hetzer and K. Wolf devised a "baby test" measuring perception, memory, body mastery, emotional reactions, social relations, and intelligence within the first year of life (Hetzer and Wolf, 1928, pp. 62–104).

Making use of such objective methods of studying hospitalism, the Vienna group of psychologists reached a number of conclusions. In 1934, H. Durfee and K. Wolf's study of 94 infants (p. 277) found that infants who were placed in institutions which emphasized only hygienic care demonstrated greater developmental retardation on special baby tests than did infants who were placed in institutions which emphasized care by the infants' own unmarried mothers, nurses, or babysitters (Durfee and Wolf, 1934, p. 305). Furthermore, spontaneous care from the infants' mothers was found to be more beneficial for the infants' health and development than care by trained staff, even when maternal care was offered by unmarried, neglected, or poorly educated mothers for whom the child was probably a burden (Durfee and Wolf, 1934, p. 312). On this basis, Durfee and Wolfe proposed that infants need love and interest and a variety of contacts with other human beings as well as bright, cheery surroundings (1934, pp. 319–320). Likewise, in 1937, I. Gindl, another psychologist from the Vienna School, used a special test to compare twenty infants raised in institutions, twenty raised in foster families, and twenty raised in their own inadequate families. Gindl found that infants left with their own families displayed overall better social, emotional, and intellectual development than infants transferred to impersonal institutions, whereas the best development was recorded from infants placed in "good" foster homes (Gindl, Hetzer, and Sturm, 1937, pp. 324–327).

Finally, in 1945, René Spitz, making use of Hetzer and Wolf's test for rating infants' behavior (Spitz, 1945, pp. 55–57), conducted the most extensive and highly controlled research thus far devised for comparing the development of institutionalized infants who received care from their own visiting mothers (institution I), and the development of institutionalized infants who did not receive attention from a mother or mother substitute (institution II). In these studies, infants from institution I, "The Nursery," were fed, nursed, and cared for by their own mothers (pp. 57 fn 1, 64), while infants from institution II, "The Foundling Home," were fed by nurses according to a ratio of one nurse attending eight infants; otherwise the infants in institution II lacked human contact for most of the day (1945, pp. 57 fn 1, 64). Both institutions were situated outside the city in large spacious gardens; both provided carefully maintained hygienic conditions; both offered the infants well-prepared food which varied according to the needs of the individual infant; both provided careful medical care. In institution I, however, infants not only received care and stimulation from their mothers, they also were afforded toys to play with and were placed in cribs where they were able to observe the hustle and bustle going on all around. Conversely, in institution II, the infants not only received deficient mothering, they also possessed no toys, and were placed in cots which were effectively screened from the world so that each baby was in solitary confinement (Spitz, 1945, pp. 62–63).

Spitz's investigation revealed a dramatic difference in the development and health of these two groups of infants. The isolated infants in institution II, infants who lacked maternal care, "showed all the manifestations of hospitalism, both physical and mental. In spite of the fact that hygiene and precautions against contagion were impeccable, the infants showed from the third month on extreme susceptibility to infection of any kind." Spitz concluded that in the institution lacking maternal care, "there was hardly a child in whose case history we did not find reference to otitis media, or morbilli, or varicella, or eczema, or intestinal disease of one kind or another" (Spitz, 1945, p. 59). At the same time, these children's developmental quotients (DQ) declined from a DQ average of 124 during the first third of the first year of life to an average of only 72 during the last third (Spitz, 1945, p. 58). In contrast, in institution I, which provided ample opportunities for maternal care and stimulation, the infants "at the end of their first year were on the whole well-developed and normal" (p. 58). Spitz went on to observe: "The problem here is not whether the children walk or talk by the end of the first year; the problem . . . is how to tame the healthy toddlers' curiosity and enterprise. They climb up the bars of the cots after the manner of the South Sea Islanders climbing palms" (p. 60). Their developmental quotient, which averaged 101.5 during their first four months in institution II, remained normal with an average of 105 four months later (p. 58).

Thus, experimental investigations supported M. Pfaundler's convictions that deprivation of maternal care for institutionalized infants was a key factor responsible for the dire symptoms of hospitalism. This conclusion, however, led researchers to wonder why infants who are deprived of maternal care soon deteriorate both psychologically and physically. In answer to this question, hospitalism or its equivalent has been variously explained in terms of (1) the predominance of sensory deprivation; (2) disruption of maternal bonding; and (3) the deprivation of empathic care. The following considerations are presented in an attempt to evaluate these explanations.

1. *Are disturbances pertaining to sensory deprivation a key source for psychological deterioration among infants deprived of mothering?* D. O. Hebb (1958, p. 110) defined deprivation as a function of a psychologically restricted sensory environment, an isolation from sensory stimulation. Langmeier and Matejcek summarized this concept as "a quantitative impoverishment which would be understood as a deficit of certain elements in the environment, [a deficit of] stimuli as such or stimuli of a specific kind, or [a deficit of] certain structuring of stimuli . . . necessary for normal development and for the maintenance of psychological functioning" (Langmeier and Matejcek, 1975, p. 13). In this sense, deprivation of infants has been understood in terms of deficient

quantity, complexity, and variability of stimuli (p. 303).

As early as 1934, Durfee and K. Wolf suggested that infants fail to receive as much stimulation within an institutional setting as they would from their own mothers or mother substitutes. These conclusions were based upon the observation that frequently institutionalized infants (1) do not receive the close physical contacts with the caretaker's body as would infants nursing at the mother's breast; (2) are rarely provided with an opportunity to play with their nurses; (3) usually share a nurse's attention with eight to ten other infants with the result that there is less time available for the nurses to contact and stimulate each infant (Durfee and Wolf, 1934, pp. 315, 319–320). These conclusions have been summarized by Langmeier and Matejcek (1975, p. 74). This hypothesis was substantiated by Sturm who compared twenty-four hour observations of children raised in an institution versus children raised in devoted homes. She discovered that the institutionalized child was given the opportunity to handle only one-seventh of the toys and other objects which the "family" child played with (Gindl, Hetzer, and Sturm, 1937, p. 350, Table 10). To a greater extent such a child was left alone during the first two years of life. Thus, within families, adults directed attention to infants an average of ninety-seven times a day during the infant's first year of life, whereas within an institution, adults directed attention to infants an average of only nineteen times a day (Gindl et al., 1937, p. 352, Table 11). Moreover, in order to maintain hygienic conditions, many institutions isolated infants. Spitz writes of such an institution, a foundling home, in which infants readily developed hospitalism. In this foundling home infants were placed in hygienic individual cubicles of glass enclosed on three sides and open at the end. The infants remained in their cubicles up to 15 to 18 months. One-half of the children were located in a dimly lighted part of the ward and it was the exception if a low stool was found in the cubicles which usually contained nothing but the child's cot (Spitz, 1945, p. 61).

The possibility that such sensory deprivation may be an underlying source for psychological deterioration among infants appears all the more likely in the light of experimental investigations among adults. In one set of experiments carried out by Heron, adult subjects were exposed to conditions of sensory deprivation over a period of several days. Each subject was placed in a soundproof room in which new and changing stimulation did not occur: each subject was exposed only to (1) diffuse, nonchanging sound derived from the droning of a motor; (2) diffuse, nonchanging light stimulation via the use of translucent eyeglasses; and (3) diffuse, nonchanging tactile stimulation provided by the use of long heavy gloves and cardboard cuffs. In response to such a lack of new, patterned, and changing stimulation, these subjects eventually became confused, failed to differentiate states of waking from sleeping, and commenced to hallucinate (Heron, 1961, pp. 8–9, 16–19). It is likely that infants, too, may deteriorate emotionally during prolonged exposure to an environment which is deficient in new and changing forms of stimulation.

Sensory deprivation as a possible basis for psychological deprivation among infants lacking mothering has been evaluated by Langmeier and Matejcek as follows: "Although the concept of deprivation as simple impoverishment of the stimulus environment has been criticized as an oversimplification and a misinterpretation of the real state of affairs . . . , in our opinion this was the first viable approach to the problem. . . . In real life, of course, the situation is . . . more complex and . . . involves deprivation at other levels" (1975, pp. 316–317).

With respect to quality of stimulation, Durfee and Wolf's studies indicate that social stimulation is more important to the infant than stimulation from activity or from inanimate objects such as toys (Durfee and Wolf, 1934, pp. 313–314). This conclusion becomes understandable in terms of the realization that a human being, unlike an inanimate vehicle, can regulate the amount of stimulation according to an infant's needs from moment to moment. Such regulation is necessary since there is an optimal level of stimulation required for each individual and beyond that threshold higher levels of stimulation may evoke negative reactions (Dember and Earl, 1957, p. 95; Hunt, 1960, p. 494; Langmeier and Matejcek, 1975, p. 306). Langmeier and Matejcek note that "the child ... should neither be over- nor understimulated nor should stimulation be too monotonous. One should ensure that stimulation be appropriate to the child's ... present level of nervous functioning which changes during the course of the day in relation to sleep, feeding, and a number of other factors" (1975, p. 366; Koch, 1957, pp. 757–765). Quality of stimulation may be of equal or greater importance than quantity. Langmeier and Matejcek conclude: "Only those who know the child intimately from day-to-day contacts can appreciate his or her specific needs, capacities, interests, idiosyncrasies, and weak points" (p. 366).

2. *Are disturbances pertaining to mother–infant bonding a key source for psychological and physical deterioration among hospitalized infants?* In 1951 John Bowlby was commissioned by the World Health Organization to account for the finding that institutional infants who are not cared for by their mothers deteriorate both psychologically and physically. In that report, Bowlby stated: "What is believed to be essential for mental health is that the infant and young child should experience a warm, intimate and continuous relationship with his [or her] mother (or permanent mother-substitute) in which both find satisfaction and enjoyment" (Bowlby, 1951, p. 11). Then he went on to say that "with the best will in the world, a residential nursery cannot provide a satisfactory emotional environment for infants and young children" (1951, p. 132). "The reasons why the group care of infants and

young children must always be unsatisfactory is . . . the impossibility of [group care] providing mothering of an adequate and continuous kind" (1951, p. 133).

Thereupon, Bowlby had the choice of emphasizing (1) the adequacy or (2) the continuity of mothering as essential for an infant's healthful development or, put in another way, he had the choice of emphasizing (1) the inadequacy of mothering or (2) the discontinuities of mothering associated with an infant's separation from a mother or loss of a mother. Eventually it was deprivation in the sense of separation which Bowlby did emphasize as the antecedent of psychological and physical deterioration among institutionalized infants. Thus Bowlby's themes of investigation emphasized *Attachment, Separation,* and *Loss,* the titles of his three-volume opus (Bowlby, 1969, 1973, 1980).

This emphasis upon separation of emotional bonds and attachments to a biological mother as a source for hospitalism, however, was in conflict with a number of other investigators' findings that disruption of mother–infant bonds does not necessarily eventuate in symptoms similar to hospitalism. These investigators demonstrated that in certain institutions infants are able to develop normally after being separated from their biological, bonded mothers. In 1949, H. Bakwin referred to a large foundling home in which the children were cared for by a large corps of women volunteers, and in which children showed normal development. In this institution he failed to find among 250 children a single clear-cut case of emotional deprivation (1949, p. 517). Likewise, R. M. du Pan and S. Roth demonstrated that fourteen children appeared to develop quite normally when they were nurtured from birth in a baby training institute where great emphasis was placed upon the need "to create a life for children as similar as possible to family life," for example, where a trainee nurse was in charge of only two to three children (1955, pp. 124–129). Conversely, other investigators began to observe that infants may remain with their bonded, but unsatisfactory, mothers yet develop symptoms of hospitalism. Kohen-Raz compared the mental scores of Israeli infants raised in kibbutzim with those of Israeli infants raised in their homes. These investigators found no consistent deficiencies in the scores of infants who had been separated from their bonded mothers (Kohen-Raz, 1968, p. 489). Likewise, Tizard's comparisons of infants reared in longterm residential nurseries in England and those reared at home, revealed no cognitive deficiencies (measured via language comprehension) among infants who had been separated from their bonded mothers (Tizard, Cooperman, Joseph, and Tizard, 1972, pp. 337, 339, 355, 356). Most recently, Kagan's intensive study of thirty-two babies who had been separated from their working mothers weekdays 8 A.M. to 5 P.M., and thirty-two babies who had remained at home with their mothers, revealed that separated day-care and home-reared children developed similarly with relation to well-controlled tests objectively measuring attentiveness, excitability, reactivity to others, attachment, and cognitive function. The infants had entered the project between the ages of three-and-a-half to five-and-a-half months and remained at the nursery school until the age of twenty-nine months. "The teacher-to-child ratio was maintained at one to three for infants and one to five for toddlers. Each child stayed with a single caretaker throughout the first thirteen to fifteen months" (Rutter, 1971, pp. 255–256; Kagan, 1980, pp. 177, 180, 192–193, 259).

Recently, Bowlby himself has returned to his original focus upon deprivation in terms of insensitive mothering rather than simply in terms of an infant's separation from a mother as an antecedent for emotional and physical deterioration (Bowlby, 1973, p. xiii; 1988, pp. 50, 125). This is a position which Bowlby had originally expressed to the World Health Organization in 1951 when he declared "a child is deprived even though living at home if his mother (or permanent mother substitute) is unable to give him the loving care small children need" (Bowlby, 1951, p. 11). Bowlby considered separation from a mother only a "partial deprivation" (1951, p. 12). This view was affirmed in 1966 when Mary Ainsworth's summary of Bowlby's views emphasized that maternal deprivation may occur when an infant remains with a mother who provides insufficient care (Ainsworth, 1966, p. 290). Thus, deprivation may occur when no separation from the biologically bonded mother has taken place. In brief, these findings suggest that the mental and physical and psychological deterioration characteristic of hospitalism is not based upon separation of bonded ties per se (Rutter, 1971, p. 255).

3. *Are chronic deficiencies of empathic care and consequent disturbances of stimulus contacts a key source for psychological deterioration among infants deprived of mothering?* Joyce Robertson reviewed the history of twenty-five pairs of mothers and infants at the Hampstead Well-Baby Clinic in London, from the period of the infants' birth until the age of three to five years, and discovered that all of the infants of twenty empathic, caring mothers developed normally and happily, but none of the infants of five emotionally unresponsive mothers developed normally (Robertson, 1962, p. 248). The symptoms displayed by infants of the unresponsive, cold, isolated, narcissistic mothers were similar to those associated with hospitalism displayed by institutionalized infants. Details pertaining to the behavior of the five unresponsive mothers and the psychological deterioration of their infants are summarized in cases 1, 2, 3, and 4 in chapter 3.

Similar findings have been reported by Coleman and Provence (1957, p. 291; see also p. 286); the Clarkes (1960, pp. 27, 29); Prugh and Harlow (1966, pp. 206–207, 210). These findings pertaining to the deterioration of infants raised by their own but unresponsive mothers contrast with the emotional health discovered among infants raised in a number of special institutions which could provide close personalized care from one or more emotionally responsive nurses (e.g., du Pan and Roth, 1955, pp. 124–129). These findings lead to the formulation that the underlying determinant of an infant's emotional health is not the presence or absence of a biological mother or of an institution per se, but rather the underlying presence or absence of consistent, empathic care (Robertson and Robertson, 1971–1972, pp. 312–313). It is the responsiveness of an empathic person (mother or substitute caregiver) with an ability to tune in to the infant's emotional communications which assures an infant the appropriate type of stimulation at the appropriate time (Steele, 1980, pp. 56, 57). This hypothesis that deprivation of empathic care during infancy is a primary factor leading to an infant's physical, cognitive, emotional, and developmental deterioration can be more fully evaluated in the light of an objective definition of empathic care, a task which the next chapter addresses.

CHAPTER 2

Definitions: Empathic Care and Deprivation of Empathic Care

EMPATHIC CARE: A DEFINITION OF "CARE"

"Care" as a component of empathic care during infancy will be defined in terms of "motherliness" or maternal affectional types of behavior which include: (1) enduring, positive pleasurable contacts with the infant; (2) watchful attention and awareness of conditions affecting the infant's activities and emotions; and (3) tenderness (Benedek, 1956, p. 272; Josselyn, 1956, p. 268). The following clinical and experimental findings reported in the psychological literature pertain to these forms of behavior which provide an essential setting for the operation of empathic care.

Persisting, Pleasurable Contacts with the Infant as Components of Maternal Affectional Types of Care

Among humans as well as among other mammals, maternal affectional types of emotional behavior can be differentiated from other well-known types of emotional reactions.

15

Aggression involves contacts of ever-increasing force and power, including destructive force; fear involves unpleasurable, negative contacts of avoidance; sexual emotions involve mounting positive, pleasurable contacts over a limited, circumscribed period of time, with a "high" of orgastic pleasurable excitement followed by a sudden reduction in excitement. On the other hand, maternal affectional contacts involve tender, positive, pleasurable contacts which evenly and continuously persist to afford the infant tranquility, comfort, and protection.

Among mammals, specific components of maternal behavior are regulated by the physiological processes within the limbic emotional–instinctual systems in the core of the brain. The ejection of milk has been found to be regulated by neural tracts leading from the hypothalamic core of the limbic brain to the posterior pituitary gland (Cross and Harris, 1952, p. 148). Furthermore, relatively small lesions higher within the limbic instinctual brain interfere seriously with grooming, litter survival, nest building and repair, as well as with protection of the young by retrieval from harmful conditions such as excessive heat. Significantly, such grooming, nesting, and nursing, as primary activities associated with the maternal instincts, all foster close and persisting, tender, pleasurable contacts between mother and infant. Some examples of these conclusions are presented by DeVore (1963, pp. 310–311) and by Jay (1963, pp. 286–288). Likewise, Harlow concludes that among the Rhesus monkeys, "contact clinging [rewarding for the infant as well as for the mother] is the primary variable that binds mother to infant and infant to mother" (Harlow, Harlow, and Hansen, 1963, p. 268).[1]

---

[1] From his experimental studies with primates, Harlow has concluded that a mother's experiences during her own infancy will be one factor as to whether she will express a positive, persisting pleasurable contact with her infants (Harlow, Harlow, and Hansen, 1963, pp. 275–276). An abused

Watchfulness, Attention, and Awareness as Components of Maternal Affectional Types of Care

Such pleasurable contacts between caregiver and infant reward the reinforcement of the maintenance and repetition of such contacts and provide an important source for the caregiver's heightened close attention in relation to the infant. Pleasurable maintenance of auditory contacts with the infant promotes careful listening, while pleasurable maintenance of visual contacts promotes careful watchfulness. Such contacts are in a position to help contribute to the caregiver's awareness of what conditions are impinging upon the infant's being and awareness of what concomitant reactions the infant is displaying. By prolonged visual and auditory contacts, as well as prolonged tactile contacts maintained by the caregiver's concomitant feelings of pleasure and reward, the caregiver gains a better chance of learning what a cry at a certain time of day may indicate and what changes the infant may be needing.

The importance of pleasure/reward reinforcement of a caregiver's attention and awareness of an infant's reactions to environmental stimulus conditions has been emphasized by Robert Emde. Emde notes that a cardinal principle of infant care, and, subsequently, a cardinal principle of therapy, involves the concept of "Be there" (Emde, 1980a, pp. 87–88), meaning be available, be an available listener, be

---

female infant becomes an abusive mother and, conversely, a female infant who has been warmly, closely, tenderly held during its period of helplessness will be likely to grow up to become a mother who contacts her own infants warmly, closely, and tenderly. The possibility arises that when a helpless female infant has received persisting positive, pleasurable contacts from her mother, the warm persisting, pleasurable emotions associated with her infancy may be retriggered when later in life she herself becomes a mother.

interested, and tune in to the infant's feelings. Mary Ainsworth has stressed this same conclusion that

> [The caring] mother must be reasonably accessible to the baby's communications before she can be sensitive to them. Accessibility is a necessary condition for sensitive awareness. . . . An inattentive "ignoring" mother is, of course, often unable to interpret correctly the baby's signals when they break through her obliviousness, for she has been unaware of the prodromal signs and of the temporal context of the behavior [Ainsworth, Bell, and Stayton, 1974, p. 128].

Tenderness as a Component of Maternal Affectional Types of Care

Tenderness (gentleness, placidity) is also a conspicuous characteristic of maternal affectional behavior among animals, whether the tenderness pertains to the behavior of a powerful tigress who gently picks up her cubs with her sharp teeth, or the behavior of a mother bird who quietly and peacefully nestles close to her young to keep them warm and protected from the elements.

The relation of soft, tender, gentle contacts on the one hand and caring attention and awareness on the other, becomes understandable in terms of the knowledge that attention to delicate cues requires a quiet, peaceful approach, much as an appreciation of fine music requires concerted peaceful attention upon the part of the listener. States of wild excitement provide a basis for aggressive attack or sexual interaction, but such excitement would interrupt sensitive awareness of the emotional responses of a fragile infant. The caregiver's *tenderness* counters a tendency to be abrupt and impulsive. It helps prevent states of overarousal and thus provides a basis for comforting the infant. The relation of tenderness to tranquilizing forms of stimulation is considered in the final section of this chapter.

EMPATHIC CARE:
DEFINITION OF "EMPATHY"

The basic core of empathy has been variously defined as "the capacity . . . to feel as the object does" (Olden, 1953, pp. 112–113); "the ability to sample other's affects . . . and to be able to respond in resonance to them" (Easser, 1974, p. 563). Empathy involves our "using ourselves, however briefly, as resonating instruments that share and reflect our subject's emotions and needs" (Karush, 1979, p. 63). It provides a basis for "experiencing in some fashion the feelings of another person" (Schafer, 1959, p. 347). Kohut notes that empathy involves "the capacity to think and feel oneself into the inner life of another person" (Kohut, 1984, p. 82). Such empathic emotional resonance has also been referred to as an emotional reciprocity (Emde, 1980a, pp. 94–95). In the same sense, Thomas and Chess employ the term consonance (contrasting with dissonance) to describe the matching or "goodness of fit" of a caregiver's response to the infant's behavior (Thomas and Chess, 1977, pp. 11, 46, 68, 204; 1980, p. 90).

During the first three months of an infant's life, empathic resonance or reciprocity necessarily has been investigated primarily in relation to the infant's excitement–quietude and pleasure–displeasure axes of emotion, since these are the only emotional responses which thus far have been able to be observed and objectively measured so early in infancy. (For a summary of the literature, see Emde, 1980b, p. 28, and 1980a, p. 99). Therefore, as the result of reciprocal activation, the mother will tend to experience the infant's states of pleasure and unpleasure as well as to experience the infant's states of arousal and tranquility. It is on this basis that *the central core of a caregiver's empathic reaction for an infant will be defined in this monograph as the capacity of the caregiver to experience pleasure in response to the infant's pleasure and to experience tender unpleasure (sadness, concern) in re-*

sponse to the infant's unpleasure. Conversely, the central core of an infant's emerging empathic reactivity will be defined as the capacity of the infant to experience pleasure in response to the caregiver's pleasure and to experience unpleasure in response to the caregiver's unpleasure.

According to this definition, a caregiver's empathy for an infant provides a basis whereby the caregiver will find mutual pleasure/reward in the infant's pleasurable behavior; that is, will reinforce the maintenance and repetition of the infant's pleasurable behavior. An example of such empathic mirroring is presented by Brazelton's experimental observations. Figure 1 below, adapted from Brazelton, illustrates the resonance with which a mother reflects and reinforces her baby's states of pleasurable attachment and arousal (Brazelton, 1980, pp. 79–80; 1983, p. 47). In connection with these findings, Brazelton notes that the empathic mother and baby are looking at each other, smiling, touching, vocalizing together (Brazelton, 1983, pp. 47–48).

An empathic caregiver will find pleasure in the infant's pleasure and will mirror rather than interfere with the infant's pleasurable rhythms (Brazelton, Koslowski, and Main, 1974, pp. 61–63). By allowing the infant to turn away, the caregiver provides the infant with a secure base from which to find pleasure in the surrounding world, thus allowing freedom for its own emerging ego. In this way, the infant is allowed the pleasures of being attached and then the pleasures of momentarily separating before it returns to a state of attachment (Brazelton, Koslowski, and Main, 1974, p. 64). When the infant's rhythm of turning toward and turning away is duplicated by the empathic caregiver, the caregiver follows the infant's pleasurable cues much as two adults, dancing in harmony, reinforce each other's pleasurable interactions (Brazelton and Als, 1979, pp. 360, Table 1,

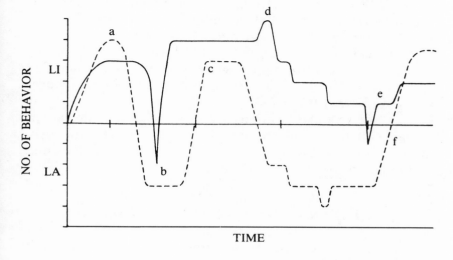

Figure 1. The mother's LI (looking intensely toward the baby) mirrors the infant's LI (looking intensely toward the mother) and the mother's LA (looking away from the baby) mirrors the infant's LA (looking away from the mother).

-------- The mother's LI and LA
_____ The infant's LI and LA

Modified from Brazelton, T. B., Koslowski, B., and Main, M., The Origins of reciprocity (The early mother-infant interaction). In: *The Effect of the Infant on its Caregiver*, (eds.) M. Lewis and L. Rosenblum, New York: 1974 John Wiley and Sons, p. 63, with permission from the authors and publishers.

21

pp. 364–365, 366–367). In contrast, the unempathic caregiver will frequently interrupt the infant's pleasurable rhythms (Brazelton, Koslowski, and Main, 1974, p. 64). Thus, the symbiotic caregiver who cannot stand a moment's rejection, as well as the controlling caregiver who must dominate the infant, both will find it difficult to permit the infant to turn away (Stern, 1974, p. 413).

Note that these various aspects of maternal affectional care—such as tender tranquilizing, pleasurable, attentive contacts—provide a peaceful sensitive background setting for the operation of empathic resonance.

THE INFANT'S NEED FOR EMPATHIC CARE

What is so special about empathic care? Why can't a conscientious parent serve an infant well by supplying a careful regime of temperature control, feeding, holding, stimulating, bathing, grooming, and diapering, without persistent positive attachments, attentive awareness, tenderness, and sensitive resonance characteristic of empathic care? Anna Freud addresses this question as she observes:

> Except when asleep the infant will tolerate rarely to be left alone. On the other hand, for the outside observer this continued presence and care . . . obscures to a large degree the true picture and extent of the infant's needs. It is . . . [the mother's] task to remove tensions as fast as they occur, and to supply satisfactions before the need for them rises to a climax of despair. The well-cared-for baby therefore appears to the outside to "need little." But with the absence of the mother who performs this service, the observer could not fail to notice that the same infant does need a multitude of things done to it, and needs them practically from morning till night and gives the environment peace only when he is at peace himself, i.e., asleep [A. Freud, 1953, p. 16].

Actually, assiduous attention to the infant's life day by day is a prerequisite for the caregiver's awareness of what conditions are arousing the infant's distress or pleasure at any given moment.

The infant's dependence upon empathic care as a source for pleasure and as a protection from distress can be best illustrated by research and clinical observations pertaining to the infant's ever-changing needs for arousal stimulation and for tranquilizing comforting stimulation.

The Infant's Ever-Changing Needs for Tranquilizing Stimulation

An adult may erroneously surmise that an infant requires a quota of stimulation in order not to be deprived of sufficient arousal, and an absence from stimulation in order to be quieted and to rest. Often a parent may not be aware that the infant's needs for stimulation are not simply a matter of the presence or absence of stimulation but rather the presence or absence of certain different categories of stimulation. For example, overexcited, agitated, upset infants who need to be sedated require not an absence of stimulation but the presence of tranquilizing forms of stimulation. From the neurophysiological point of view, this formulation is summarized by Diamond and his colleagues as follows:

> In the infant–mother dyad, the mother or her surrogate is more than a resource for the infant's basic needs for food, warmth, shelter, and cleansing, more even than a resource for love and social learning; she is also an important resource for stimulations which are an essential aid to the infant's still inadequate inhibitory capacities. At birth, the human organism is remarkably ill-equipped to cope with the variations and excitations of its new environment. It is a subcortical creature, which is in danger of going into shock through over-

reacting to powerful or unexpected stimuli because it lacks the means for modulation of behavior which is made possible by development of cortical control. The role of the higher structures is played by the mother: she is the child's auxiliary cortex. She does this through various acts of tactile stimulation and handling which are included in the pattern of mothering, such as cuddling, stroking, shifting positions, and grooming. These serve to reduce over-reaction and to mobilize the infant's inhibitory capacity. The emotionally healthy mother performs these acts or their equivalents spontaneously. For example, the infant at birth responds to a sudden noise with a Moro [startle] reflex and startle reactions. The psychological component of the startle reaction is fright. . . . A responsive mother reacts smoothly and quickly to the stimulus of the loud noise by making gentle, physical contact with the infant, with the intent to diminish its reaction. When the reaction has already taken place, she will perform any one of a number of acts which help to relax the infant, such as rocking it, stroking it, uttering her soothing phrases or placing her hand on the infant's body [Diamond, Balvin, and Diamond, 1963, pp. 305–306].

Benjamin notes that especially during the third and fourth weeks of life, sensitivity to external stimulation increases to the point that infants tend to be overwhelmed unless a mothering person acts as a tension-reducing agent (Benjamin, 1961, pp. 19–42; cited by Korner, 1964, p. 68). Also, Margaret Ribble concluded from her clinical observations of infant care that infants respond to certain rhythms and mild intensity of proprioceptive and tactile stimulation in the form of cradle rocking or auditory stimulation in the form of a lullaby in the first months of life in order to establish a satisfactory pattern of sleep (Ribble, 1965, pp. 47–48, 59). Such tranquilizing stimulation also is needed when an infant is excessively aroused, disturbed, or irritated.

    In general, tranquilizing stimulation is gentle, soft, and tender and is characterized by: (1) *diminishing intensity* such as is afforded by a mother talking or singing more and more quietly *to* her infant until the infant drifts off to sleep; (2) *diminishing rhythm rates*; for example, patting, rocking, and talking to the infant at a rate initially matching the infant's own movements and then becoming slower and slower as the infant's excitement gradually subsides (Bowlby, 1969, pp. 293–294); (3) *deep pressure,* gently and diffusely applied; (4) *gradualness of change* temporally and/or spatially; for example, gradual changes in intensity of stimulation, gradual changes in rate of stimulation, gradual changes in configuration of stimulation (in contrast to changes that are highly demarcated and sudden). Whereas suddenly demarcated temporal and spatial change provides a basis for sharpness and roughness, spatial and temporal gradualness and diffuseness combined with reduced intensity provides for tranquility and sleep (Wolff, 1966, p. 44).[2]

On the other hand, as the months go by, an infant requires an increasing degree of arousal stimulation as a source for stimulation of consciousness, alert wakefulness, and the development of the infant's sensorimotor, emotional, and cognitive capacities.

The Infant's Ever-Changing Needs for Arousal Stimulation

Stimulation which arouses states of alertness and excitement involves: (1) *increases in the intensity* of tactile, visual, auditory, or proprioceptive stimulation; (2) *suddenness in temporal*

---

[2] Diffuse, gentle, rocking rhythmic stimulation which tranquilizes the infant reflects the type of stimulation to which the embryo is exposed in utero: the uterine amniotic fluids serve to reduce the intensity and suddenness of a forceful blow to the surface of the mother's body and provide for the lapping, oceanic motions of gentle repetitive and diffuse stimulation for the fetus.

change in tactile, visual, auditory, or proprioceptive stimulation as occurs during playful movements; (3) *suddenness in spatial change*, for example, provided by sudden changes in visual and tactile forms and shapes; (4) an *increasing speed* of tactile, auditory, and/or proprioceptive stimulation as occurs during playful hugs, tickling, and laughter. If arousal stimulation becomes too intense, then comforting, tranquilizing stimulation is required in order to moderate mounting distress.

Within a given range, an infant's need for arousal and tranquilizing stimulation actually varies from one time of day to another and even from moment to moment (Brazelton, 1969, p. 50). For example, after a long day, an infant may become tired and irritable, at which time he or she requires tranquilizing stimulation in the form of tender comforting to reduce inner states of irritation and to induce a state of tranquility and sleep. On the other hand, an hour or so after waking, a healthy active baby is not ready for tranquilizing sleep-inducing forms of stimulation but rather for playful arousal stimulation which reinforces the activation of wakeful muscular activity and cognitive receptivity (Stern, 1974, pp. 404, 405, 406). At any given time, one should be able to plot degrees of pleasure as a function of arousal and tranquilizing stimulation. Within a given range of arousal stimulation at any given time, the infant experiences reactions of pleasure and reward, whereas at intensities above and/or below this range, the infant displays discomfort and distress (Stern, 1974, p. 411). Likewise, within a given range of tranquilizing stimulation at any given time, the infant experiences reactions of pleasure and reward, whereas at intensities below or above this range, the infant displays signs of discomfort and distress. Bouncing and tickling an infant who needs to sleep leaves the infant in a state of helpless frustration. So would sleep-inducing monotonous rocking of an infant who is ready to expend an abundance of healthy energy. Thus, the parental ego is allotted the difficult task of distributing to the infant mild forms of arousal stimulation at certain times and mild forms of tranquilizing stimulation at other times, to fit the infant's constantly changing requirements. These, then, are some of the reasons why the infant's need for stimulation as a source for pleasure and a protection from distress is not a matter of how much stimulation in general should be offered but *what kind* of stimulation *at what time.* A critical question then arises as to whether the caregiver can respond appropriately to the infant's expression of its needs.

In brief, these examples pertaining to an infant's ever-changing needs for various types of stimulation draw attention to the conclusion that no simple fixed prescription can tell an adult how to fulfill an infant's needs from moment to moment and how to relieve the infant's ever-changing conditions of distress. These examples therefore suggest why, throughout its waking hours, an infant requires the benefits of all aspects of *empathic* care (persisting, positive, tactile, visual, and auditory attachment; attention; tenderness; and empathic, resonant, emotional awareness) if it is to be consistently protected from mounting distress and if its rewarding states of pleasure are to be facilitated and maintained.

DEPRIVATION OF EMPATHIC CARE DURING INFANCY: SOME DIRECT AND INDIRECT DEFINITIONS

Column 1 of Table I outlines the definition of empathic care in relation to the observations presented in chapter 2. Conversely, column 2 of this table reciprocally draws attention to the definition of deprivation of empathic care.

However, when information pertaining to empathic deprivation is uncertain, deprivation may have to be judged indirectly in relation to the caregiver's emotions.

TABLE I

DEFINITION OF EMPATHIC CARE FOR INFANT	DEFINITION OF DEPRIVATION OF EMPATHIC CARE FOR INFANT
1. Enduring pleasurable emotional attachment to infant	1. Lack of enduring pleasurable emotional attachment to infant
1a. Persisting, positive, pleasurable contacts (tactile, visual, auditory) with infant	1a. Lack of persisting, positive, pleasurable contacts (tactile, visual, auditory) with infant
1b. Persisting attention to infant via tactile, visual, auditory contacts	1b. Lack of persisting attention to infant via tactile, visual, auditory contacts
2. Tenderness, a basis for tranquilizing and comforting infant	2. Lack of tenderness toward infant, lack of tranquilizing and comforting infant
3. Resonant distress whereby the infant's unpleasurable distress activates the empathic caregiver's tender comforting protection	3. Lack of resonant distress whereby the infant's unpleasurable distress fails to activate the caregiver's tender comforting protection

Since the emotions of hate, anger, disgust, dissatisfaction, fear, depression, withdrawal, and frozen affect run counter to resonance with an infant's pleasurable feelings, the diffuse presence of such emotions in the caregiving person would provide indirect indications of empathic deficiencies. Furthermore, an adult's verbal admission of one or more of these negative emotions of hate, anger, disgust, dissatisfaction, fear, depression, and withdrawal specifically directed toward a given infant would be assumed to indicate disturbances with respect to an adult's capacity for relating to an infant empathically (i.e., to support the infant's states of pleasure and to reduce the infant's states of unpleasure).

Mary Main lists some "aloof," "unapproachable" positions which a caregiver may display toward an infant, positions which suggest deficits of empathic care. Some indices of aversion are as follows:

1. Keeping the head at a different level from the infant's, or making no effort to align the head with the infant's, when this would be appropriate.
2. Keeping the body midline angled away from the infant.
3. Keeping the shoulders back rather than curved toward the infant.
4. Keeping the knees up or in some other position so that there is no opportunity for the infant to reach the lap/chest/stomach.
5. Failing to shift posture to "follow" the infant's movements.
6. Arching back or away at the infant's approach.
7. Moving the neck and head back uncomfortably while holding the infant.
8. Moving into or remaining in uncomfortable postures, the relaxation of which would bring the parent into contact with the infant.
9. Folding the arms across the stomach as though to prevent the child's body from touching the parent's ventral

surface, especially when the child is seated upon the parent's lap.
10.   Wincing or flinching as the child moves into closer contact [Main, 1990, p. 487].

Furthermore, if empathic care of an infant involves maintenance of conditions that activate the infant's pleasure and interruption of conditions that activate the infant's distress, then deprivation of empathic care could be predicted via observation of an adult's (1) increased tendency to interrupt pleasurable conditions and (2) an increased tendency not to interrupt distressful conditions.

The following references to cases described in the literature disclose often hidden aspects of such forms of empathic care deprivation.

Case 1: Brody and Axelrad's Case "Z" (1978, pp. 21–22)[3]

Brody and Axelrad write of the problems faced by an infant when its mother interrupts the infant's pleasurable activities. The moment the baby pauses in his sucking at the mother's first breast, the mother gently changes his position, interrupts his pleasurable nursing, and instead offers him cereal she has already prepared.

[Thereupon] he is slow to take the food from the spoon and swallow it. He fusses, his breathing becomes more rapid and he appears to labor at a task that taxes his resources far more than sucking at the breast did a few minutes before. . . . The mother says she has to offer the cereal in the midst of breast feeding because otherwise the baby fills up on milk and takes no semi-solids. . . . The baby's restlessness grows until the mother also becomes tense; she then resumes the breast feed-

---

[3] Since Brody and Axelrad gave no numbers to these cases, the symbols "Z" and "Y" will be used to facilitate referencing.

ing. But the baby's sucking is not smooth, his body is less relaxed, his hands and toes are clenched. The mother is silent and looks uneasy and disappointed. He has taken hardly any cereal.

The mother appears more concerned that she has not been able to force her baby to take the cereal rather than being interested in whether her baby's nursing is a happy experience.

Case 2: Brody and Axelrad's Case "Y" (1978, p. 44)

Brody writes of interrupted pleasure among infants within an institutional setting: "The younger and less experienced [nurses], especially those stationed in crowded areas, were usually more busy and hurried and showed less concern with the baby's physical comfort. Some had strict rules about the need to burp, for example, every 30 seconds, or after every few sucks, and had no hesitation about suddenly interrupting the neonate's sucking arbitrarily for this purpose." Burping was more important than maintaining the infant's tranquil, contented nursing. The infant's pleasure did not activate the nurse's empathic feelings of pleasure and induce her to linger over this peaceful activity.

Case 3: Brody and Axelrad's Case of Mrs. Crane and Cathy (1978, pp. 80–81)

A case in which an infant's pleasure in being held was abruptly terminated without tenderness was described as follows by Brody and Axelrad: Mrs. Crane picked up the baby and put her down rather abruptly.

I [Dr. Brody] mentioned my observation, asking if it seemed

to her correct—I knew she was very busy and would not intentionally handle a little baby abruptly. I was probably right, she said. I asked whether at the end of the feedings, instead of quickly rising and placing the baby in the crib [sudden interruption and interference with pleasurable activity] Mrs. Crane might take time to talk with Cathy a little [maintaining some of the pleasurable contact]: the slower transition might ease [tranquilize] Cathy's distress and help her fall asleep peacefully in her mother's arms.

Case 4: Sally Provence's Case of Mrs. "A"
(1983, p. 238)

Conversely, Provence describes the typical case of a mother who did not seek to interrupt the distressful conditions to which her infant was exposed: "Anne, at three months, cried intensely when hungry. It later became clearer that Mrs. A could not mobilize herself to feed the baby at the first signs of hunger and gave the bottle only after Anne's crying was prolonged and intense." Although Mrs. A "dressed the baby nicely for the social worker and enjoyed showing her off . . . [she] left her strapped on the bath table and was unresponsive to her crying." The mother was unresponsive, that is, expressed no empathic discomfort in observing the infant's intense discomfort.

Case 5: Khantzian and Mack's Case of Bill
(1983, p. 219)

Khantzian and Mack write of a parent's failure to interrupt conditions leading to an infant's impending harm:

[Eighteen-month-old Bill] would actively bolt around the large conference room. . . . He was noted to pick up anything on the floor that appeared "mouthable" whether edible or otherwise, and put it in his mouth. He frequently stumbled, banging various parts of his body, usually his head. . . . Unfortunately, his father usually was not one of those who was alarmed by and concerned about Bill's behavior and injuries.

Father did not display empathic care in terms of interrupting these harmful activities or attempting to provide tranquilizing stimulation to comfort the child.

CHAPTER 3

Deprivation of Empathic Care During Infancy: A Source for Chronic Loss of Pleasure

Symptoms associated with deprivation of empathic care during infancy can be analyzed in terms of the two emotional axes which have been reliably measured during early infancy: the arousal excitement–lethargy axis and the hedonic pleasure–displeasure axis (Emde, Kligman, Reich, and Wade, 1978, pp. 134–136; Emde, 1983, pp. 180–181). This chapter focuses upon deprivation of empathic care as an antecedent for states of deficient pleasure or reciprocal distress. Chapter 4 will focus upon deprivation of empathic care as an antecedent for *HYPER* and *HYPO States* of arousal.

As a background for understanding the effects of chronic losses of pleasure in response to prolonged deprivation of empathic care, Section 1 of this chapter focuses upon the positive processes whereby empathic care serves as a persisting supply line for maintaining and enhancing the infant's states of pleasure. Conversely, Section 2 focuses upon the negative processes whereby deprivation of empathic care is followed by the infant's loss of pleasure.

EMPATHIC CARE: A BASIS FOR MAINTAINING THE INFANT'S STATES OF PLEASURE AND FOR REDUCING THE INFANT'S STATES OF DISTRESS

The infant's pleasure can be operationally measured in terms of his or her smiles, cooing, gurgling; the presence of playful movements of the limbs; and the presence of pleasure–reward reinforcement of the maintenance and repetition of the infant's contacts; for example, reward reinforcement of the infant's eye contacts, auditory contacts, and tactile contacts with its caregiver.

Conversely, the infant's displeasure or distress can be measured in terms of crying, screaming, screeching, frowning, flailing, squirming, breath-holding, and by an increase in central nervous system reactions typical of those found in the presence of noxious stimuli and punishment. These include an increase in the infant's negative reactions of turning away, for example, turning away from visual and/or auditory and/or tactile contacts or from emotional mirror-resonance with the caregiver. In extreme cases, the infant may completely withdraw with a negative extinction of all emotional contact.

With the assistance of these definitions of the infant's pleasure and distress, the following hypotheses are presented as a basis for assessing and predicting the relation between an infant's supply of empathic care, the maintenance of the infant's states of pleasure, and the reduction of the infant's states of distress.

Hypothesis 1:

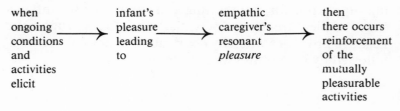

| when ongoing conditions and activities elicit | → | infant's pleasure leading to | → | empathic caregiver's resonant *pleasure* | → | then there occurs reinforcement of the mutually pleasurable activities |

Hypothesis 2:

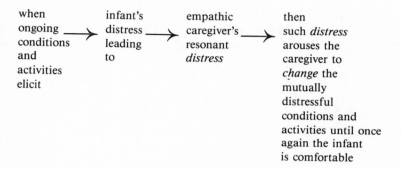

when ongoing conditions and activities elicit → infant's distress leading to → empathic caregiver's resonant *distress* → then such *distress* arouses the caregiver to change the mutually distressful conditions and activities until once again the infant is comfortable

Additionally, clinical and experimental studies have demonstrated that not only can an empathic caregiver's pleasure be resonantly activated by an infant's pleasure, but also an infant's pleasure can be resonantly activated by a caregiver's pleasure. Likewise, not only can an empathic caregiver's distress be resonantly activated by an infant's distress, but also an infant's distress can be resonantly activated by a caregiver's distress. Daniel Stern writes: "resonant emotional response is the core of the empathic experience . . . built into the central nervous system and functioning from very early in [the infant's] life" (Stern, 1983, p. 83; Lipsitt, 1984, p. 83). In the same vein, Steele notes that "the infant tends to reproduce the affect and behavior of its caregiver (1983, p. 242). Such affective resonance may possibly be based upon an inborn genetically determined response system. Kestenberg and Buelte conclude that the infant can attune to the mother's rhythms (1983, p. 207) and Peter Wolff uses the term *infectious* to refer to this capacity for infants to pick up the emotions of others (1987, pp. 222–223). Among toddlers and older children, Anna Freud and Dorothy Burlingham, as early as 1942, reported on their studies of children's emotional reactions to the German bombings of London during World War II. They concluded that when a

mother shook and trembled in response to the aerial bomb-
ing, the infants and children also shook and trembled. Conversely, when a mother responded cheerfully that the
children could go out to play in the yard as soon as the bombings were over for the day, the children in turn responded
cheerfully without distress (A. Freud and Burlingham, 1942,
pp. 279–280). More recently, Emde has experimentally demonstrated how a mother's states of pleasure as well as her tender, muted distress can be transmitted to the infant (Klinnert,
Campos, Sorce, Svejda, Emde, 1983, pp. 66, 67, 68). In
Emde's studies, twelve-month old infants who were placed
in a position of uncertainty as to whether they should crawl
from a secure location to a position which was less secure
were guided by the emotions of their mothers' faces. When
the mothers displayed happy faces as the infants moved forward toward the less secure location, 74 percent, or fourteen
of the nineteen infants, crossed to the less secure side (i.e., the
mother's emotion of pleasure was conveyed to her infant and
thereby reinforced the maintenance of the infant's ongoing
behavior). In contrast, when the mothers of seventeen infants displayed fearful expressions, none of the infants
crossed to the less secure side (i.e., the mother's emotion of
distress was conveyed to her infant and thereby disrupted the
infant's ongoing behavior) (1983, pp. 184–186).[1]
    Emde's experiment demonstrates how the transmission

---

[1] These experimental findings provide a key answer to the questions
"How do you teach infants and children right from wrong?" "Don't you
have to use punishment?" The answer to these questions, of course, is that
infants and children can learn from empathic resonance as demonstrated
by Emde's and by Anna Freud's findings. Infants and children who can
resonate with their caregiver can respond to the caregiver's pleasure via
reciprocal pleasure which in turn reinforces and rewards the maintenance
and repetition of their ongoing behavior. Conversely, infants and children
who can resonate with their caregiver can respond to their caregiver's
tender states of unpleasure with reciprocal unpleasure which in turn
serves to disrupt (i.e., to change) their ongoing behavior.

of muted distress from an empathic caregiver to an infant provides a basis whereby the infant can be protected from impending harm and consequent serious distress: the empathic caregiver's anticipatory distress can activate the infant's distress and thereby result in the infant stopping a potentially dangerous course of action.

Demos emphasizes how the capacity of an empathic caregiver to respond in resonance to an infant's pleasure, together with the capacity of the infant to respond in resonance to the caregiver's pleasure, provide a basis for a reverberating pleasure cycle which reinforces the infant's states of pleasure and pleasurable activities (Demos, 1984, p. 18).

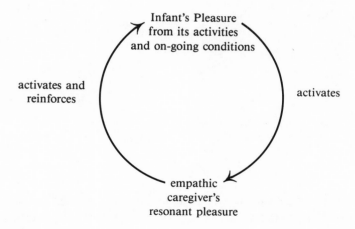

Figure 2. The infant's pleasure activates the caregiver's resonant pleasure, thus initiating a mutually reinforcing pleasure system.

At the same time, the caregiver's pleasurable attachment to her infant, a primary aspect of empathic care, can be conveyed to her infant and once again can set in motion the reverberating caregiver-infant pleasure cycle:

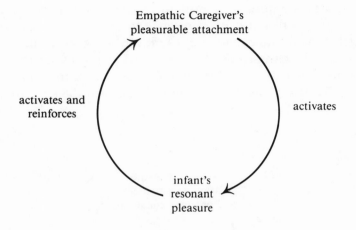

Figure 2a. The caregiver's pleasure activates the infant's resonant pleasure thus initiating a mutually reinforcing pleasure system.

In this way the infant and the care it receives from its caregiver almost realize a single system or unit. The reciprocal sequences between infant and caregiver under optimal conditions, establish a "mutuality" (Erikson, 1968, p. 219) or "coherence" whereby infant and caregiver progressively mesh their various cycles and "fit together" (Sander, 1983, p. 337).

According to these formulations, an empathic caregiver's positive pleasurable contacts with an infant provide a rewarding background to reinforce an infant's ongoing sociable, cognitive, and motor activities (e.g., to reinforce the infant's walking and talking, cuddling or listening, exploring or playing, and to foster its interest in nature and in people) (Winnicott, 1963a, p. 223; 1963b, p. 239).

On the other hand, the capacity of a caregiver to react empathically with distress in response to an infant's distress might be expected to prove detrimental: the caregiver's resonance with the infant's distress might be expected to overwhelm the infant by reinforcing his or her distress were it not for the caregiver's capacity for empathic tenderness. Tenderness, it is proposed, converts the caregiver's resonant distress into tender distress, or concern. In such a case, the caregiver's caring, tender contacts serve as a source for comforting and soothing the infant, while at the same time the caregiver's muted distress serves to motivate the caregiver to interrupt and change the distressing condition (see Figure 3).

Thus, an infant's distress becomes a resonance motivating an empathic caregiver to contact the infant tenderly and to keep making changes until the infant is comfortable; i.e., the distress becomes a basic form of infant communication which says "please change what is happening" (Emde, Gaensbauer, and Harmon, 1976, pp. 85, 87). Conversely, the infant's pleasure becomes a process of resonant pleasure which reinforces (rewards) an empathic caregiver's maintenance and/or repetition of ongoing conditions and becomes a basic form of infant communication which says, "Keep up what you are doing, I like it, [please continue]" (Emde et al., 1976, p. 87). Stated in another way: empathic care favors interruption of the infant's distress but opposes interruption of the infant's pleasure.

There are instances, however, in which an empathic caregiver will be prevented from reinforcing an infant's pleasurable activities or may even find it necessary momen-

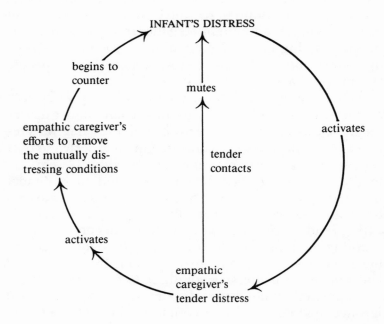

Figure 3. The infant's distress activates the caregiver's resonant tender distress thus initiating the caregiver's corrective and comforting behavior.

tarily to directly expose the infant to distressful conditions. For example, the empathic caregiver may have to interfere when an infant is playing with a dangerous toy or interrupt an infant when he or she is eating a hurtful substance. Furthermore, the empathic caregiver may have to subject the infant to painful injections of penicillin or place the infant in an orthopedic brace. In such cases, anticipatory distress may motivate the caregiver to protect the infant from prolonged future distress. However, the caregiver's empathic responsiveness can be conveyed to the infant by means of tender comforting which would reduce the traumatic, overwhelming effects of the infant's exposures to painful procedures and losses (Demos, 1984, p. 20).

DEPRIVATION OF EMPATHIC CARE: A BASIS FOR AN INFANT'S CHRONIC LOSS OF PLEASURE

The findings outlined in Table I in chapter 2 suggest that the caregiver's enduring warm, gentle, pleasurable attachment to the infant provides a basis for the following components of empathic care as an essential supply line of the infant's pleasure:

1. The caregiver's persisting visual, auditory, and tactile contacts with the infant as a source for pleasurable attention;

2. The mutual pleasure-resonance between caregiver and infant as a source of pleasure;

3. The caregiver's tenderness as a basis for pleasure;

4. The caregiver's resonant tuning in to the infant's distress as a basis for protection, comforting, and pleasure.

Conversely, an infant's chronic deprivation of empathic care amounts to the infant's chronic loss of these supply lines of pleasure. This section focuses upon these chronic losses of pleasure among deprived infants. The following clinical findings reported briefly by Joyce Robertson (1962, pp. 245–264), and those reported at length by Sally Provence (Ferholt and Provence, 1976, pp. 439–459), illustrate the chronic loss of pleasure displayed by infants chronically deprived of empathic care. Robertson's findings are based upon the Hampstead Nursery records of infants deprived by their disinterested mothers as compared to the Hampstead Nursery records of infants who had not been deprived. Robertson found that no chronic losses of pleasure were displayed by twenty infants who were cared for by warm empathic mothers. On the other hand, chronic loss of pleasure appeared among the following four infants who, for long periods of time, were deprived of empathic care.

Case 6: Robertson's Reference to Peter
(1962, pp. 249–250)

Chronic Deprivation of Empathic Care During Infancy:[2]
Peter's "mother handled him competently but appeared harassed and depressed. She was conscientious, devoted to her son, and pleased with his development. But she was an unhappy woman, seriously *inhibited in her ability to express feeling or to witness it in others.*" The mother "*did not talk to her baby or play with him*" and displayed inadequate comforting (p. 249; emphasis added).

Chronic Loss of Pleasure:
"Peter first smiled at about six weeks, but did not progress to the free smiling which is typical of babies between two and three months. When talked to, he would listen and look, move his limbs and head and lips but only rarely would the expected smile appear. . . . In the waiting room, mother and child would sit silent and still like two wooden figures" (p. 249). "Peter always looked healthy but there was no animation or pleasure in his body movements or in his facial

---

[2]This description of Peter's depriving mother is also presented in Case 19.

expression." At three years, in nursery school, "Peter makes a queer impression with his rapid alternations of joyous excitement and inhibition. Even his expressions of joy seem somehow unnatural and inappropriate to his age or to the occasion" (p. 250).

Case 7: Robertson's Reference to Maurice
(1962, pp. 251–253)

Chronic Deprivation of Empathic Care During Infancy:[3]
"[T]he behavior which characterized this mother was her imperturbability and the detached way in which she could discuss Maurice's difficulties: . . . it was puzzling that she could not give him the comfort he so badly needed" (p. 252).

This mother displayed no signs of pleasurable attachment for her infant. She "did not fondle or kiss" Maurice (p. 253). "Bodily contact did not come easily to her and was kept at a minimum" (p. 253). "Remoteness and lack of empathy affected her ability to answer even the physical needs of her babies. . . . Her aloofness, her rigid control of feeling, her avoidance of body contact, and lack of empathy meant that she was unable to meet the needs of her children on many levels. . ." (p. 253).

Chronic Distress with Loss of Pleasure:

> Maurice was a baby who cried from birth. . . . At three months he was in a hospital for twenty-four hours accompanied by his mother to have a hernia repaired. . . . By five months he was overwhelmed by anxiety, screaming at everything and everybody and this typified his behavior for the rest of the first year. . . . To offer a toy or even to look at him was to

---

[3]This description of Maurice's depriving mother is also presented in Case 18.

risk provoking the most excruciating screams. . . . When he
eventually walked and talked . . . his movements were slow,
stiff and overcautious, and he held his head and shoulders in
an abnormally tense way. His movements lacked pleasure
and spontaneity [pp. 251–252].

Case 8: Robertson's Reference to Mary
(1962, pp. 254–256)

Deprivation of Empathic Care During Infancy:[4]

Mary, the first child, was breast-fed for two and a half months,
but it was not a success. The mother reported that she disliked
feeding the baby and the baby did not enjoy it either. . . . From
the very beginning the mother was aware that she was dissatisfied and unhappy with Mary and got no pleasure from
her. . . . By the time Mary was a year old, the mother was comparing her unfavorably with every other baby she saw and
rejecting her by word and gesture.

The mother sabotaged the clinic's effort to help her to stimulate and cathect the baby. "For instance, when it was suggested that Mary needed company, the mother put her for long
periods in the front garden where she could see passersby
and later when Mary needed scope for free movement, the
mother emptied a room of furniture and left her there by herself" (pp. 254–255).

Chronic Loss of Pleasure:
"Mary was a beautiful baby, but at seven months her large
watchful eyes were expressionless and her mouth drooped
unhappily; she showed no pleasure in anything" (p. 254).

---

[4]This description of Mary's depriving mother is also presented in
Case 20.

Case 9: Robertson's Reference to Beatrice
(1962, pp. 250–251)

Chronic Deprivation of Empathic Care During Infancy:
The "mother was conscientious but lacking in intuition, warmth, and identification with her baby. The work with her consisted largely in trying to make her aware of the baby's needs. In a limited and unintuitive way, she did much of what was suggested to her, but it was impossible to invest her care with feeling" (p. 250). "And when Beatrice wanted attention —wanted to be lifted from the floor, for instance—[the mother] would look away to avoid responding" (p. 251). The mother reported that Beatrice, at the age of seven and a half months, "was happiest when left alone in her cot or pram." She therefore "never took her shopping or for walks. She left the child unsupervised in the garden for long periods, even while she went to the hairdresser or dentist" (p. 251).

"This mother did not fulfill the [tender] role of comforter. When her child cried, for instance, after an injection, it called out no response. She would look away from Beatrice and continue talking" (p. 251).

Chronic Loss of Pleasure:
"At three months, baby and mother made a curious impression of dullness. They would look at each other silently with expressionless faces" (p. 250). "At six months [the infant] was serious and her looking had a staring, intense, and apprehensive quality. She looked with interest at toys and was aware of the person offering them, but she showed no pleasure and rarely any movement toward them. A glimmer of a smile appeared very occasionally" (p. 251).

Similar findings are reported at greater length in two in-depth studies by Ferholt and Provence (1976, pp. 439–459) and by Provence (1983, pp. 233–256). The following case presentations 10 and 11 summarize these findings.

Case 10: Ferholt and Provence's Mrs. J
(1976, pp. 439–459)

Chronic Deprivation of Empathic Care During Infancy:
Mrs. J's father fell ill with leukemia two weeks after her wedding. Several weeks later he died (p. 441). When shortly thereafter she became pregnant, Mrs. J wanted an abortion. She pleaded with her medical consultant that she was unable and unwilling to be a mother. Nevertheless, against her will, she was forced to complete her pregnancy and to deliver an infant boy (p. 441). Anxious as well as depressed, she became frustrated by what she perceived as the infant's lack of communication and felt that the baby was intentionally rejecting her (p. 442). The mother held the infant awkwardly and turned away from her baby (deficiency of positive contacts) (p. 443). She did not admire her baby's body and did not spend relaxed times cuddling, kissing, patting, rocking, or arousing him; the only vigorous stimulation which the baby received from her occurred when she scrubbed him and changed his clothes after he would regurgitate (p. 444). The infant's only happy time occurred once a day when the father would frolic with him. However, the father often became moody and withdrawn (p. 442).

Chronic Loss of Pleasure with Reciprocal Distress:
This infant who lacked empathic care demonstrated a chronic deficiency of sustained pleasure and an excess of distress. He almost never smiled and almost never showed pleasurable excitement (p. 443). At best, he displayed subdued pleasure if he was tossed in the air (p. 443). His facial expressions, vocalization, or body movements hardly ever appeared joyful or excited (pp. 445–446). He became listless and displayed distress monotonously and continuously (p. 442). He became withdrawn, and when his withdrawal was interrupted he resorted once again to a position of irrita-

bility (p. 442). Worst of all, his gastrointestinal system responded negatively with distress by rejecting food: he spit up thirty times each day. No organic cause for this behavior could be found (pp. 440, 444). The baby became hypoactive in spite of adequate gross motor coordination (p. 445). He spent little time enjoying, watching (p. 443), listening to, or touching the outside world (minimal pleasurable maintenance of tactile, visual, or auditory contacts) (p. 446) and displayed very little self-stimulation (p. 444). He displayed no positive pleasurable interest in age-appropriate toys (p. 443). These states of deficient pleasure and excess distress primarily were not determined by inexorable constitutional defects but rather were related to the infant's deprivation of empathic care: the boy recovered when he was treated therapeutically by being put into the sensitive hands of a single primary caregiver and was given periods of affectionate, tactile, kinesthetic stimulation including hugging, kissing, stroking, rocking, and passive exercise (p. 451). With this treatment, his pleasure increased, he began to show activity, his vomiting ceased, and his weight developed normally to reflect physically the growth of a healthy and happy baby (pp. 449–451, 453–454).

Case 11: Provence's Mrs. A and Baby Anne
(1983, pp. 233–256)[5]

Chronic Deprivation of Empathic Care During Infancy:
With respect to the pleasurable close attachment aspects of empathic care, baby Anne was severely deprived from the start. Mrs. A complained that during delivery her baby "tore her apart" (p. 235). "This was the first of many comments over

---

[5]Provence's presentation is an elaboration of a case initially incompletely reported by Ernst Kris at the time of his death (Kris, 1962, pp. 175–215).

the next two years in which she characterized the infant as aggressive and damaging to her; and this statement antici- pated the battle ahead. On the first day she found the baby beautiful but by the second day she began to refer to her as unattractive" (p. 235). Furthermore, Mrs. A "reported that she did not pick up baby Anne often or hold her more than very briefly for fear she would spoil her" (p. 236). During baby Anne's two-month visit, the clinic staff "noted Mrs. A's problems in holding and cuddling her baby. She was ob- served to give the infant the bottle while holding her at a dis- tance across her lap" with minimal body contact (p. 236). Unfortunately, Mrs. A's emotional feelings toward Anne continued to worsen. By the time Anne was five months old, Mrs. A was depressed to the extent that she was "unable to find pleasure in caring for the baby; she could not enjoy feed- ing her or making the feeding experience . . . gratifying for the baby," neither could she make other experiences gratifying (p. 241). Besides being depressed, Mrs. A became bored, lonely, angry, and guilty (p. 243).

Mrs. A was only minimally able to use the advice she received from her worker who was seeking to help her care for Anne (p. 244). Mrs. A "was aware of being bored and could verbalize her boredom but was unaware of the cursory and cold quality of her contacts with Anne." At the time of Anne's eight-month check-up, there were increasingly fewer of Anne's experiences that Mrs. A could mutually enjoy (p. 244) even though "Anne had made considerable adaptation to the nongratifying and threatening environment" (p. 244). "The absence of playful social interaction . . . was especially poignant" (p. 245).

Mrs. A gave Anne her bottle only after Anne's crying was prolonged and intense. "It later became clearer that Mrs. A was unable to make any feeding fully satisfying and pleasant for Anne" (p. 238). Mrs. A's inability to be motivated by ten- der concern for Anne's states of distress was also illustrated by the indifference she displayed when she left Anne alone and crying, helplessly strapped to the bath table (p. 238).

However, the most malignant aspects of little Anne's deprivation of empathic care derived from Mrs. A's rage at Anne's unhappy crying. She would then spank Anne hard "to give her something to cry about" (pp. 238, 241, 245). Mrs. A reacted to Anne's distress with angry distress rather than with tender distress and comforting (pp. 238, 241, 243). Figure 4 illustrates the vicious cycle whereby an infant mirrors a caregiver's angry distress and the caregiver mirrors the infant's angry distress, a vicious cycle which was not alleviated by means of tender comforting. Demos draws attention to such a negative spiral (Demos, 1984, p. 26).

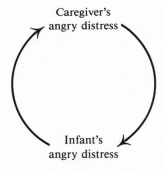

Figure 4. The caregiver's anger activates the infant's anger and the infant's anger reinforces the caregiver's anger.

Chronic Loss of Pleasure with Reciprocal Distress:
Baby Anne's reactions to such chronic deprivation of empathic care did not appear for the first few months of her life

when she was receiving some supportive care from her aunt. However, by the age of three-and-a-half months, her chronic loss of pleasure made its first appearance. Thus, "As a newborn, Anne was described by the observers as an unusually pretty and well-formed infant who ate and slept well and was normal in every way. She was responsive in all sensory modalities and was especially alert visually. A moderately active infant who nestled easily into the arms of the adult, she was promptly quieted when restless, by being held and cuddled" (pp. 234–235). Furthermore, during Anne's first two months of life, when Anne was being taken care of by her mother's helpful and caring sister-in-law, Anne's physical and emotional health was found to be excellent. Her examination at the well-baby clinic revealed that Anne was "alert and responsive with an excellent balance of receptivity and reactivity and an unusual ability in perceptual discrimination. She smiled responsively to the face of adults and visually followed both persons and toys. She reacted to social stimulation by cooing and other vocalization" (p. 236).

Then, at the time of her six-month check-up, little Anne increasingly evidenced a reduction in pleasure. Her loss of pleasure first became manifest in relation to inanimate objects whereby there gradually appeared less and less pleasure-reward reinforcement of the maintenance and repetition of her contacts with her toys (p. 241). By the age of seven and three-quarter months, Anne distressfully showed more vigor in getting rid of her toys than in obtaining them, reactions typical of unpleasure and punishment rather than reactions of pleasure and reward (p. 242).

More serious, by that time she displayed clear signs of distress at the approach of her mother and an anxiousness which subsequently pervaded her behavior with strangers (p. 243); her smile soon showed signs of unhappiness "in that it often had the quality of a grimace" (p. 246). Her attachment to Mrs. A continued to deteriorate and at her ten-and-a-half month visit to the clinic, it was noted "contact with the examiner and with her mother appeared weak and poorly sustained" (p. 247), a sign of insufficient pleasure-reward reinforcement of her contacts with mother and generalized with others. The most dramatic sign of little Anne's chronic state of displeasure was her disturbed crying. By the time of her seven and three-quarter month visit, Anne displayed screaming spells at home, spells lasting ten or more minutes (p. 243) and toward the end of the first year Mrs. A complained of Anne's "screeching" at night in her crib. At the age of one year, Anne cried for almost an hour during her visit to the well-baby clinic and could not be comforted by anyone, the mother or the pediatrician. "The crying had a desperate, intensely unhappy quality." In the words of Ernst Kris, "observers . . . found themselves watching a child who could not be reached or comforted but was left to her own uncontrollable despair" (Kris, 1962, p. 212; Provence, 1983, p. 248).

An unempathic caregiver may eventually "come around" to taking care of an infant's hunger and/or thirst, cuts, bruises, rashes, stomachaches, colic, constipation, nasal congestion, choking, excessive heat or cold, sleeplessness, and dangerous positioning. Yet, when the infant's physical needs are finally met after delayed withholding of gratification, the infant often has become so unhappy and distraught that distress and lack of pleasure are carried over into the period of actual physical care. Expressed in other words, there is little to assure that the unempathic caregiver will interrupt disturbing conditions before the infant has become severely distressed and depleted of pleasure.

In summary, this chapter has focused upon theory and clinical observations that account for numerous manifestations of chronic loss of pleasure and reciprocal distress displayed by infants deprived of empathic care. Among the signs which indicate such a loss of pleasure are the following:

1. A reduction in the frequency of smiling, cooing, gurgling;

2. A reduction in the pleasure–reward reinforcement of the infant's positive visual, auditory, and tactile contacts (e.g., eventuating in a deficiency in eye contact, and a deficiency in auditory contact, and/or a reduction in positive tactile contact and attachment);

3. Reciprocal increase in the frequency of frowning, crying, squirming, and screaming;

4. Reciprocal increase of negativism, including an increase of turning away physically and/or emotionally from the caregiver and from other human beings.

These preliminary conclusions based upon theory and clinical observations direct attention to the need for still further investigation of deprivation of empathic care during infancy as an antecedent for chronic loss of pleasure.

CHAPTER 4

Deprivation of Empathic Care During Infancy: A Source for *HYPER* and *HYPO States* of Behavior

Clinical studies have drawn attention to the conclusion that chronic deprivation of empathic care during infancy is followed by not only chronic loss of pleasure but also numerous *HYPER*[1] and *HYPO*[1] *States*. *HYPER States* include one or more of the following:

1. *HYPER States* of consciousness and wakefulness (Goldfarb, 1943, p. 263; Greenspan, 1981, pp. 240–241).

2. *HYPER States* of exaggerated amounts of random activity and increased speed of activity (Goldfarb, 1943, p. 263; Langmeier and Matejcek, 1975, p. 318; Money, 1980, p. 370; Greenspan, 1981, pp. 242–243).

3. *HYPER States* involving the exaggerated emergence of repetitive, rhythmic behavior such as rocking, thumb sucking, masturbation, and headrolling (Ribble, 1965, p. 60).

---

[1]The terms *HYPER* and *HYPO* are presented in upper case italics in referring to the author's conceptualization of these states. In other cases, the terms "hyper" and "hypo" are presented in lower case format in quoting directly or indirectly from the literature.

4. *HYPER States* of exaggerated sensitivity and reactivity to stimuli (Bergman and Escalona, 1949, pp. 335–352; Langmeier and Matejcek, 1975, p. 318).

5. *HYPER States* of muscular tension, stiffness, rigidity, and exaggerated intensity of muscular force (Robertson, 1962, pp. 250, 251, 252; Greenspan, 1981, p. 240).

6. *HYPER States* of exaggerated visceral activities, for example, involving increased pulse, increased rate of respiration, increased speed of eating, frequency of urination and defecation (Spitz, 1951, pp. 262, 263, 265, 267).

Conversely, *HYPO States* include one or more of the following:

1. *HYPO States* of reduced arousal of consciousness characterized by somnolence and lethargy (Spitz, 1951, p. 271; Ribble, 1965, pp. 51, 52, 78, 117; Langmeier and Matejcek, 1975, p. 318; Greenspan, 1981, p. 240).

2. *HYPO States* of reduced quantity of movement and/or reduced speed (Spitz, 1951, pp. 270–271; Langmeier and Matejcek, 1975, p. 318; Money, 1980, p. 370).

3. *HYPO States* of reduced sensitivity and reactivity to stimuli (Ribble, 1965, pp. 51–53; Langmeier and Matejcek, 1975, p. 318).

4. *HYPO States* of muscular flaccidity and reduced muscular force (Spitz, 1951, p. 271; Robertson, 1962, p. 247; Ribble, 1965, pp. 6–9; Langmeier and Matejcek, 1975, p. 318).

5. *HYPO States* of reduced visceral activity, for example, involving reduced heart rate, reduced respiratory rate, reduced amount and speed of eating, reduced frequency of urination, and/or reduced frequency of defecation (Ribble, 1965, pp. 6–7).

These expressions of hyper and hypo levels of arousal during infancy parallel the processes of the "diffuse, non-specific activating system" of the brain and its ascending and descending irradiations from the base of the brain up to the cerebral cortex as well as down to the total body musculature (Magoun, 1958, pp. 25–33). This system has been found to regulate:

1. Hyper and hypo diffuse ascending excitation of consciousness and wakeful behavior ranging from excited consciousness to states of lethargy and sleep (Moruzzi and Magoun, 1949, p. 471; Lindsley, 1952, pp. 443–456, Table 1; Magoun, 1958, p. 33).

2. Hyper and hypo diffuse descending tonic activation of generalized increased tone and tension of the somatic musculature (French, 1960, p. 1291).

3. Hyper and hypoactivation of rhythmic behaviors such as turning, swinging, rocking, crawling, walking, talking (e.g., Ward, 1957, pp. 266–267; Delgado, 1967, p. 66).

4. Hyper and hypo states of sensory sensitivity (French, 1960, pp. 1300–1301).

5. Hyper and hypo states of visceral activation, for example, affecting arterial pressure, peripheral motor tone, respiration, galvanic skin reflexes and reactions of the gastrointestinal tract and "indeed upon all phases of autonomic balance" (French, 1960, pp. 1299–1300).

In brief, the *HYPER* and *HYPO States* evidenced among infants deprived of empathic care reflect the processes of the nonspecific arousal system of the brain. Over the years such effects of deprivation during infancy have been denoted by many different names. Money has used the terms hyperkinesis and hypokinesis (1980, p. 370). Bergman and Escalona have focused upon deprived infants, their "sensitivities," their "over-excitability," and their "violent reactions" (1949, pp. 336, 337, 346). Goldfarb and then Langmeier have spoken of hyperactivity and hypoactivity to refer to such states of hyper- and hypoarousal (Goldfarb, 1943, pp. 250, 263; 1944, p. 163; Langmeier and Matejcek, 1975, pp. 318, 326).

CLINICAL FINDINGS

As early as 1935, Lauretta Bender became aware of children who presented a picture of "infantile asocial hyperkinetic behavior," "a common experience of early emotional deprivation" based upon institutionalization or ever-changing placements in foster homes (Bender, 1935, cited by Bender; 1975, p. 436). Shortly thereafter, in 1938, William Goldfarb reported his conviction of a relation between the exposure of infants to impersonal institutionalization and the emergence of hyperactivity. He conducted a controlled study in 1943 to investigate this clinical impression (Goldfarb, 1943, pp. 258, 259, 261, Tables VI, VII, X). He compared the symptomatology of (1) a group of forty children who were interned within an institution from early infancy until the age of three years when they were placed in foster homes; and (2) a control group of forty children who from the beginning had been raised in foster homes (1943, p. 251, 252, Table I). In contrast with the institutionalized infants, the foster home infants in this study, for the most part experienced close and consistent care from early infancy (1943, p. 264). According to the findings of this study, the institutionally raised children displayed hyperactivity twice as frequently as did the infants raised in more caring foster homes (Goldfarb, 1943, p. 261, Table X; 1944, p. 162). In relation to such findings, Langmeier and Matejcek in 1975 hypothesized that the infant who has been deprived of mothering "initially attempts to restore the interrupted environmental contact by increased [diffuse] activity" as occurs among experimental animals who have become hyperactive when deprived of food; long-term or permanent and total deprivation, however, leads to a drop in arousal level, i.e., to general hypo-activity (1975, p. 317).

More recently, John Money at the Johns Hopkins School of Medicine has reported similar observations among severely deprived infants. In referring to *HYPER* and *HYPO States* of emotionally deprived infants, Money employed the terms hyperkinesis and hypokinesis. He described hyperkinesis as a state which is "manifested as too much motion or activity, including talk, much of it agitated, poorly coordinated, and without consistency of purpose. It is commonly characteristic of the rehabilitation phase through which abused. . . [children] pass after separation from the agents of their abuse. For a while, their hyperkinesis may simulate hypomania. It may be punctuated by a relapse or reversion to an episode of apathetic or depressive hypokinesis" (Money, 1980, p. 370).

As indicators of early deprivation of empathic care, such *HYPER* and *HYPO States* have been observed to permeate all levels of developmental function. Thus, Greenspan contrasts (1) normoactivity among infants who have received empathic care versus (2) hyperactivity and hypoactivity among infants who have failed to receive empathic care at various stages of development (1981, p. 239). See Table II.[2]

Additionally, Margaret Ribble, René Spitz, and Joyce Robertson have individually reported detailed clinical case

---

[2]Table II uses Dr. Greenspan's framework in describing the infant's emotional patterns. The term "normo activity" has been substituted for Dr. Greenspan's term "adaptive" and the terms "hyperactivity" and "hypoactivity" have been substituted for Dr. Greenspan's term "maladaptive" (Greenspan, 1981, pp. 239–243). This presentation has been granted Dr. Greenspan's permission. Dr. Greenspan's research, which was initially presented in 1981 (pp. 239–243), is further elaborated in his texts *Infants in Multirisk Families* (1987), *The Development of the Ego* (1989), and *Infancy and Early Childhood* (1992).

TABLE II

Greenspan's Model of Ego Development with Superimposed Effects of Early Deprivation:
Maladaptive Hyperactivity/Hypoactivity, Distress and Loss of Pleasure

Infants' Age	Normoactivity (Adaptive)	Hyperactivity (Maladaptive)	Hypoactivity (Maladaptive)
0-3 months	Relaxed; sleeps at regular times; cries only occasionally. Is very alert; looks at one when talked to; brightens up when rocked, touched, or otherwise stimulated.	Rigid, becomes completely distracted by any sights, noises, touch, movement; always upset and crying.	Spends most of the day sleeping; shows no interest in anything or anyone; does not respond to stimuli.
2-7 months	Very interested in people, especially mother or father; looks, smiles, responds to their voices, their touch with signs of pleasure.	Insists on being held all the time; will not sleep without being held [demands for tranquilizing contacts].	Uninterested in mother, father, or other primary caretakers (e.g., always looks away rather than at people); withdrawn.
3-10 months	Able to interact in a purposeful manner; smiles in response to a smile; able to get involved with toys . . . and have pleasure when interacting with a person.	Demands constant interaction; has temper tantrums or withdraws if caretaker does not respond to his signals.	Seems oblivious to caregivers; does not respond to their smiles, voices, reaching out.
9-24 months	Manifests a wide range of socially meaningful behavior and feelings. Can play or interact with parents. Able to go from interacting to separation and reunion with organized affects including pleasure. Can explore new objects and new people.	Behavior and affect completely random and chaotic. Toddler almost always appears "out of control" with aggressive affects predominating.	Rarely initiates behavior; mostly passive and withdrawn; compliant.

material to demonstrate the emergence of *HYPER* and *HYPO* somatic and visceral states following severe deprivation of empathic care during infancy. The following illustrative case material reflects the findings of these clinicians as well as the author's.

THE DISPLAY OF HYPER STATES
AMONG INFANTS DEPRIVED OF EMPATHIC CARE

Case 12: Ribble's "Baby Rob" (1965, pp. 48–49)

HYPER States:
   [Baby Rob] was ten months old when he was referred to . . . [Margaret Ribble's] study group because of what his mother called a "peculiar rolling habit." He had apparently been a very good sleeper from the time of birth, but the mother had discovered, on coming home late one night, that the infant was rocking violently back and forth in the bed with his arms tightly clasped around the end of the blanket. Observation showed that this was a regular occurrence. She was greatly disturbed and immediately jumped to the conclusion that the baby had somehow been injured and that, as she put it, "there was something mentally wrong with the child" [p. 48].

Deprivation of Empathic Care During Infancy:
   In giving information about the general development and routine care of this infant, [the mother] repeatedly emphasized the fact that she had never played with him, that he had never been rocked or jiggled, and that he had always been left alone in his own bed in the nursery to go to sleep by himself. The nursery, she insisted, was "perfectly quiet, and entirely isolated from the rest of the house" [p. 49].

   When the suggestion was made to the mother that it would be good for her to spend a few minutes while holding and play-

ing with the child at regular intervals before his feedings during the day, and particularly in the later afternoon, she was
plainly horrified and explained that she had taken special
care "not even to let the [infant's] father see him late in the
afternoon when he came home from business lest the baby
become too excited." She was willing, however, to try the
experiment of rocking the infant to sleep at night to test the
result. She also agreed to place a dim light in the nursery, so
that if the child was restless he need not waken in a totally
dark room [p. 49].

The rolling habit, of course, did not immediately disappear
under this treatment, but there was enough improvement in
the general reactions of the infant within a week to convince
the mother that she should continue the procedure. With the
dawning understanding of what was wrong with her baby,
this mother, who was not only intelligent but loving, worked
out an ingenious scheme for supplying the appropriate
stimulation which was so greatly needed.

Two months later, at the end of the infant's first year, she
reported that the rolling habit had entirely disappeared [p.
49].

Case 13: Ribble's "Baby Sally" (1965, p. 61)

Acute Deprivation of Empathic Care During Infancy:
The infant initially was breast-fed and cared for only by her
mother, and developed well for the first four-and-a-half
months of her life.

At this time the mother was suddenly called away from the
home and the baby had to be weaned abruptly. The . . . [in-
fant] was left in the charge of an aunt who gave her the most
conscientious care, exactly as it had been prescribed by a

pediatrician. [However], for fear that the infant would be handled too much, the aunt had been instructed not to pick her up; accordingly, she did not hold the baby for bottle feedings or fondle her.

Acute HYPER States:
During the first week of the mother's absence, no noteworthy reaction was observed. The ... [infant] did not cry and apparently slept very soundly at night. However, a marked pallor developed in spite of scrupulous hygienic attention to fresh air, sunlight, and diet. By the end of the second week, the aunt was horrified to discover that when going to sleep the ... [baby] rolled her head violently, at times knocking it on the side of the crib. Not long after this she began to bang her head with her fists during the day, at times picking at her hair. This behavior continued off and on for a period of two months. Finally, in desperation, the aunt decided that a psychiatrist must see the child because she had the idea that some serious nervous disorder had developed. In the meantime, the mother had returned, and it was not difficult to outline a course of treatment [of picking the infant up with tender care during nursing, of playing, comforting, etc.] which she carried out in an excellent and even exaggerated fashion, so that the ... [baby] rapidly recovered, soon being restored to an entirely normal condition.

Such an emergence of *HYPER States* among infants who have suffered a deprivation of empathic physical contacts and care has also been reported by Weil. The following case summaries from *Instinctual Stimulation of Children*, Volume 2, provide further illustrations of *HYPER States* in the form of head banging, rocking, head rolling, increased locomotor motility, as well as in the form of tenseness, rigidity, and screaming temper tantrums appearing among infants deprived of empathic care.

Case 14: Weil's Case of "Leon"
(1989b, Case 44, p. 177)[3]

Deprivation of Empathic Care During Infancy:
Leon's mother was troubled from the start. Leon's "mother's pregnancy was not a happy one. She commented: 'I gnawed inside from the moment I conceived until I delivered the baby.' And . . . a letter from the psychiatrist who treated her when Leon was two years old indicated that from the time of Leon's birth, the mother suffered symptoms of depression, crying spells, and weight loss. Her depression [a basis for withdrawal] had become more and more intense during Leon's infancy until he approached the age of two" (the age at which the mother's own sibling had died).

Chronic HYPER States:
In turn, "from the time Leon could crawl he was hyperactive; he would bang his head against the refrigerator and hurt himself. Also, he would bite his forefinger [a source of arousal stimulation] until finally the finger became 'misshapen'."

Case 15: Weil's Case of "Jerry"
(1989b, Case 76, p. 315)

Deprivation of Empathic Care During Infancy:
Jerry's mother was unable to enjoy her baby; she was too preoccupied with her own emotional problems. During her pregnancy, she took "an overdose of Librium as a 'suicidal gesture' in an effort to get people to notice her. Jerry, at the age

---

[3]The findings presented in the following cases of Weil were obtained at the time of family treatment many years after the infants had been deprived. Therefore, only outstanding details of the past events were remembered and reported.

of six months, was left in a foster home" where there was only one caregiver to care for the needs of ten infants.

Chronic HYPER States:
"By the time Jerry was about a year old, he would bang his head on anything hard, the floor, the sink, etc. Eventually, the head banging ceased, only to be replaced by his incessant 'running around like crazy,' a symptom which still continued at the time of his referral" to the clinic when he was four years old. Apparently, what arousal stimulation was not offered Jerry by his caregiver was replaced by self-arousal stimulation supplied by his own head banging and hyper-locomotion.

Case 16: Weil's Case of "Stewart"
(1989b, Case 86, p. 362)

Deprivation of Empathic Care During Infancy:
As an unwanted infant, Stewart was deprived of the pleasure-attachment aspects of empathic care.

> Six months after Stewart's mother married, she had a miscarriage. She felt that the miscarriage would not have taken place had it not been for her husband's constant sexual demands during her pregnancy. The husband, who had been exposed to his own mother's prostitution, apparently was not in a position to limit his driven sexuality even when his wife ... became pregnant with Stewart. Therefore, when Stewart was born, the mother was tired and angry. The father continued with his excessive sexual demands but offered no help to his wife while she tried to care for the baby. The mother soon could not tolerate the father *or* the baby.... [The] mother honestly stated that she always rejected [Stewart] ... and never had been able to enjoy him.

Chronic HYPER States:
"By the age of four months, Stewart would scream every night supposedly with 'colic'.... Stewart became a hyperactive

child. Even when he entered school, he could not sit still; rather, he would leave his desk during classroom lectures to walk around the classroom."

THE DISPLAY OF HYPO STATES
AMONG INFANTS DEPRIVED OF EMPATHIC CARE

The following illustrations from the clinical investigations of Margaret Ribble and those of René Spitz draw attention to *HYPO* somatic and visceral functions among infants deprived of empathic care.

Case 17: Ribble's Baby Pat (1965, pp. 51–53)

Deprivation of Empathic Care During Infancy:
Pat "had practically no mothering and was not even held for feeding." "The mother, a successful actress, was averse to breast-feeding. She weaned [the infant] suddenly at the age of four weeks and placed [her] on infrequent bottle feedings. The actual food supply was entirely adequate insofar as bulk and caloric intake were concerned but sucking time was too short" (p. 51). The bottle, propped on a pillow, would usually slip to the floor with a crash (p. 52).

Chronic HYPO States:
Pat demonstrated "a slowing up of all sensory reaction with a pronounced diminution of reflex excitability and a consequent depression of all body function. This child became extremely pale and lethargic" (p. 51). She tended to sleep the greater part of the time and if the nipple of her bottle of milk became stopped up or the flow of milk lessened she would

immediately doze off to sleep without any protest reaction (pp. 51, 52).

As would be expected for any infant who demonstrated a hypoactive arousal of consciousness and wakefulness, Pat displayed a learning problem. "At the age of six months she was retarded in many aspects of her development" (p. 51).

Significantly, Dr. Ribble reports "the engagement of the services of an extremely motherly nurse" made possible a reversal of Pat's deteriorating condition. However, "it was several months before the sensitivity of this infant was restored and her stimulus–response mechanism readjusted to healthy functional activity" (p. 53).

Spitz's Research

Such individual clinical findings of Margaret Ribble were confirmed by the quantitative studies of René Spitz. Spitz observed that the intensity of an infant's *HYPO* (depressive) *States* varied according to: (1) the number of months the infants received responsive, personal care prior to subjection to emotionally depriving conditions; and (2) the number of months the depriving conditions were maintained. Infants who had remained with their "responsive" mothers for the first six months of their lives displayed less pathology than infants who had remained only three months with their "responsive" mothers (Spitz, 1951, pp. 269–271). Thus, in one study of 170 children, thirty-four children received a minimum of six months satisfactory relations with their mothers but had to be shifted to an unsatisfactory mother substitute (a source for deprivation of empathic care). Among these cases, the infants demonstrated "a clinical picture which was progressive from month to month" (1951, p. 270). By the third month of deprivation, restriction of motility became generalized. Additionally, at this time, the infants withdrew from social contacts. After the third month of deprivation, the infants were overcome by states of lethargy and eventually became retarded in their ability to learn (1951, p. 270).

Similarly, in a study of ninety-one cases of infants who were emotionally deprived in a foundling home after only three or four months of satisfactory care with their mothers, Spitz discovered the emergence of the following signs of even more severe hypo-functioning:

> The picture of motor retardation became fully evident. The infants became completely passive, lying in their cots in a supine position. . . . The face became vacuous, eye coordination defective, the expression often imbecilic. . . . The progressive deterioration and increasing infection-liability led, in a distressingly high percentage of these infants, to marasmus and death [Spitz, 1951, p. 271].

The Display of Both HYPER and HYPO States Among Infants Deprived of Empathic Care

In chapter 3, Joyce Robertson's four-year study of the Hampstead Well-Baby Clinic's records of twenty-five mothers and their infants was cited in relation to the absence of pleasure among infants deprived of empathic care. In this chapter, these same cases are cited in relation to the occurrence of *HYPER* and/or *HYPO States* among such deprived infants. Robertson observed that none of the children of twenty empathic mothers displayed *HYPER* or *HYPO States*. However, each of the children of the five unempathic, depriving mothers did display both *HYPER* and *HYPO States*, as illustrated by the following examples (Robertson, 1962, pp. 246–264).

Case 18: Robertson's Reference to "Maurice"
(1962, pp. 251–254)

Chronic Deprivation of Empathic Care During Infancy:[4]
"The behavior which characterized ... Maurice's mother
was her imperturbability and the detached way in which she
could discuss Maurice's difficulties: ... it was puzzling that
she could not give him the comfort he so badly needed"
(p. 252).
      This mother displayed no signs of pleasurable attach-
ment for her infant.

> [She] did not fondle or kiss Maurice [p. 253]. Bodily contact
> did not come easily to her and was kept at a minimum [p. 253].
> Remoteness and lack of empathy affected her ability to an-
> swer even the physical needs of her babies. ... Her aloofness,
> her rigid control of feeling, her avoidance of body contact,
> and her lack of empathy meant that she was unable to meet
> the needs of her children on many levels... [p. 253].

HYPER and HYPO States:
"Maurice was a baby who cried from birth" (p. 251). "By five
months he was overwhelmed by anxiety and screaming" (p.
252). At nine months, his movements were slow and stiff ...
and he held his head and shoulders in an abnormally tense
way" (p. 252). However, these *HYPER States* would be replaced by *HYPO States*: thus, "at nine months Maurice could
grasp and put things to his mouth but was flabby and
moved his limbs very little. ... His movements were slow"
(p. 252).

---

[4]This description of Maurice's depriving mother has already been presented in Case 7, chapter 3.

Case 19: Robertson's Reference to Peter
(1962, pp. 249-250)

Chronic Deprivation of Empathic Care During Infancy[5]:
Peter's "mother handled him competently but appeared harassed and depressed. She was conscientious, devoted to her son, and pleased with his development. But she was an unhappy woman, seriously inhibited in her ability to express feeling or to witness it in others." The mother did not talk to her baby or play with him and displayed inadequate comforting (p. 249).

HYPER and HYPO States:
Peter, who was followed at the Hampstead Well-Baby Clinic from the age of a few weeks to the age of three years, would watch like "a petrified animal—eyes staring, body tense and stiff" (p. 250). When he was excited he displayed "a habit of standing rigid, trembling, and making unusual hand and finger movements" (p. 250). At alternate times, these *HYPER States* were replaced by *HYPO States*: "Peter always looked healthy, but there was no animation ... in his body movements. In the consulting room, he sat silently on his mother's knee" (p. 250). "Inadequate comforting led, in his case, to the gradual development of an exceptional ability to control his tears when in pain. He would tremble, flush, screw up his eyes, and swallow his tears. By the time he was a year old, this meager response had gone; even injections did not make him cry" (p. 249). "He is passive and watching rather than doing or responding" (p. 250).

---

[5]This description of Peter's depriving mother has already been presented in Case 6, chapter 3.

Case 20: Robertson's Reference to Mary
(1962, pp. 254–256)

Deprivation of Empathic Care During Infancy[6]:
"Mary, the first child, was breast-fed for two-and-a-half months, but it was not a success. The mother reported that she disliked feeding the baby and the baby did not enjoy it either. . . . From the very beginning the mother was aware that she was dissatisfied and unhappy with Mary and got no pleasure from her. . . . By the time Mary was a year old, the mother was comparing her unfavorably with every other baby she saw and rejected her by word and gesture" (p. 254). The mother sabotaged the clinic's effort to help her to stimulate and cathect the baby. "For instance, when it was suggested that Mary needed company, the mother put her for long periods in the front garden where she could see passersby and later when Mary needed scope for free movement, the mother emptied a room of furniture and left her there by herself" (pp. 254–255).

HYPER and HYPO States:
Mary, who was followed at the Hampstead Well-Baby Clinic from early infancy to three years, seemed more hypersensitive and hyperreactive perceptually than a baby should be and was "too aware of the changing mood and expression of the adult" (p. 254). In addition, she hyperactively turned to sucking, masturbating, and rocking (p. 255). However, these *HYPER States* were matched by *HYPO States* of resignation: her large watchful eyes became expressionless and her mouth drooped. Her development was slow and dull (p. 254).

---

[6]This description of Mary's depriving mother has already been presented in Case 8, chapter 3.

NEUROLOGICAL AND BIOCHEMICAL FACTORS ASSOCIATED WITH HYPER AND HYPO STATES AND LOSS OF PLEASURE

In order to understand the emergence of *HYPER* and *HYPO States* during infancy, it is appropriate to consider the following findings from the psychological literature with respect to both genetic and environmental sources for such behavior.

Genetic and Organic Determinants of Hyperactivity

In the 1920s and 1930s, Hohman (1922, p. 372), Ebaugh (1923, p. 89), and Bond and Partridge (1926, pp. 95–96) directed attention to "hyperactivity and impulsivity" with "irritability," "restlessness," "sleeplessness," "overtalkativeness" and "tics" as an organic derivative of Von Economo's encephalitis which affected large numbers of children during the early part of the twentieth century (for a reference summary, see Cohen, Shaywitz, Young, and Shaywitz, 1982, p. 205). Next, in 1937, Bradley observed that hyperactive symptomatology among children responded favorably to the administration of amphetamines (Bradley, 1937, p. 578).

This interest in hyperactivity among infants has continued to grow through the present time. Organic sources for hyperactivity among infants and children continue to be investigated in relation to: minimal brain (cerebral) dysfunction (Clements and Peters, 1962, pp. 185, 196; Morrison and Stewart, 1971, p. 189; Cantwell, 1972, p. 414; Morrison and Stewart, 1973, p. 888; Cantwell, 1975, pp. 275–276); and attention deficit disorders (Cohen, Shaywitz, Young, and Shaywitz, 1982, pp. 198–221). For an overall summary of such findings, see Bender (1975, pp. 427–436).

Thomas and Chess have stressed the importance of activity level thresholds as constitutional determinants of temperament affecting the interactions of infants with their caregivers, a basis for the emergence of behavior disorders (1977, pp. 21–22, 37, 46, 132–137). In this regard, Cohen has proposed an interactive rather than a linear model of development. Endowment (e.g., as a source of hyperreactivity or hyporeactivity) "shapes experience and in turn experience modifies the expression of endowment" (Cohen et al., 1982, p. 215). Cohen adds: "In our research, constitutional variables have been the major domain of intervention. . . . However, it is equally possible that . . . particular styles of parenting, stress, and other experiences in a child's life in interaction with biological endowment may lead to temporary or prolonged alterations in neurotransmitter metabolism" and in this way activate the infant's states of hyperactivity and hypoactivity (Cohen et al., 1982, p. 216).

Interactions of Environmental and Instinctual Biochemical Processes as Determinants of Chronic HYPER and HYPO States

Lately, investigators have begun to focus upon the dynamic environmental influences which contribute to the etiology of hyperactive states (van der Kolk, Boyd, Krystal, and Greenberg, 1984, pp. 125–126). Environmental as well as genetic pathways can provide a basis for hyperactive behavior.

This formulation is in keeping with the findings of van der Kolk, and of Maier and Seligman, and of Stone, who investigated the posttraumatic stress syndrome involving the following sequence: helpless exposure to stress precipitates a temporary or permanent disturbance of brain chemistry involving numerous neurotransmitters, and in turn, these changes are followed by the emergency of hyperactivity (van der Kolk, 1987, p. 67) or hypoactivity characteristic of "learned helplessness" in which the subject "gives up"

(Maier and Seligman, 1976, p. 3; van der Kolk et al., 1984, pp.125–126).

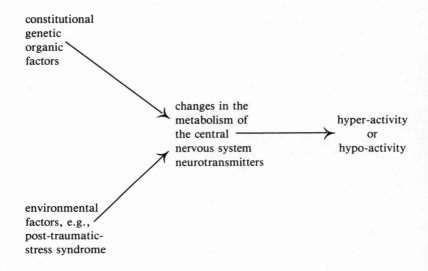

constitutional
genetic
organic
factors

changes in the
metabolism of   hyper-activity
the central   or
nervous system   hypo-activity
neurotransmitters

environmental
factors, e.g.,
post-traumatic-
stress syndrome

It has been known for a long time that exposures to stress precipitate emergency visceral activation of adrenalin from the medulla of the adrenal gland (Cannon, 1939, p. 228)—a basis for temporary hyperactivity as an emergency reaction. Now current investigations indicate that prolonged helpless subjection to stress is accompanied also by increased metabolism of noradrenalin and dopamine within the circuits of the emotional core of the brain, a basis for more permanent activation of hyperactivity. More specifically, Stone has investigated infant deprivation of maternal care as a source for the posttraumatic stress syndrome involving changes in brain chemistry and consequent hyperactivity and hypoactivity (Stone, Bonnet, and Hofer, 1976, pp. 242, 247, cited by Hofer, 1983, p. 230).

In brief, these researchers observed the following findings:

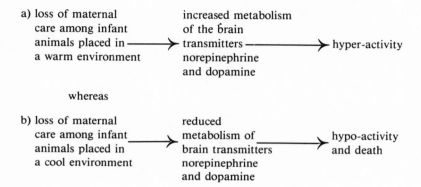

a) loss of maternal care among infant animals placed in a warm environment → increased metabolism of the brain transmitters norepinephrine and dopamine → hyper-activity

whereas

b) loss of maternal care among infant animals placed in a cool environment → reduced metabolism of brain transmitters norepinephrine and dopamine → hypo-activity and death

More specifically, Stone et al. have pointed out that rat pups that were rejected at the age of 10 to 12 days but kept warm (room temperature 35°) were able to survive. But rat pups rejected at the same age and kept cool (room temperature 23°) died within six days. The rat pups that were kept cool "showed a virtual arrest of growth of the tail, tibia, femur, and failed to increase in brain weight" (Stone et al., 1976, p. 242).

Interactions of Environmental and Instinctual Biochemical Processes as Determinants of Chronic Loss of Pleasure Among Infants

A beginning has been made with respect to investigating the effects of early deprivation upon the neurochemical transmitters of the instinctual brain not only in relation to the chronic activation of *HYPER* and *HYPO States* but also in relation to chronic loss of pleasure. The following formulations presented in Figure 5 suggest that the enkephalin early deprivation ⟶ Bonnet, Hiller et al, 1976, p. 338 ⟶ chronic reduction in the number and receptivity of the endogenous opioid neurotransmitter system of the brain:

a basis for chronic loss of pleasure accompanying early deprivation (see Belluzzi and Stein, 1977, pp. 556-558)

see summary of literature by van der Kolk 1987, p. 44 ⟶ reciprocal chronic activation of the noradrenergic neurotransmitter system of the brain:

a basis for distress accompanying early deprivation

Figure 5. Pleasure and loss of pleasure in relation to the opioid neurotransmitter systems of the brain reacting to early states of deprivation.

neurotransmitter substances of the opioid system of the brain directly or indirectly mediate reactions pertaining to pleasure and loss of pleasure in relation to early deprivation.

Van der Kolk's findings suggest that these organic effects are liable to be fixed: "There is . . . evidence that social isolation [deprivation] directly affects the number or sensitivity of brain opiate receptors . . . during critical stages of development. In one study, social isolation in young mice was found to cause decreased brain opiate receptor binding" (van der Kolk, 1987, p. 41; citing Bonnet, Hiller, and Simon, 1976, p. 338).

Similarly, Myron Hofer concludes: "Hidden within the interactions between infant and mother, we and others have found a number of processes by which the mother serves as an external regulator of the infant's behavior, its autonomic physiology, and even the neurochemistry of its maturing brain" (Hofer, 1983, p. 199).

Chronic deprivation as a source for disturbances in the infant's brain chemistry (that in turn provide a source for disturbances of pleasure and unpleasure and of *HYPER/ HYPO States* of arousal) becomes all the more understandable in the light of the fragile instability of the infant's homeostatic physiological regulatory mechanisms. One hopes that symptomatic effects arising from deprivation of empathic care during infancy will continue to be investigated via objective measurement of the infant's neuropharmacological reactions as well as the behavioral signs of the infant's loss of pleasure and *HYPER/HYPO States*. In this way, steps possibly may be taken early enough to prevent the establishment of long-range pathology.

CHAPTER 5

Deprivation of Empathic Care During Infancy: Compensatory Supply Lines of Pleasure

Lipsitt has decried the fact that "given the human is capable of experiencing and being affected by pleasures and annoyances from early infancy, precious little attention seems to be invested today in the ontogeny of pleasure reception and pleasure seeking" (1984, p. 83). Similarly, Rochlin observed that "much attention has been paid to the pain which losses or failures produce, but their obverse, the restitution and creativity they generated, have been accorded too little notice" (1965, p. 127).

In this regard, chronic losses of empathic care can be studied via either of two different approaches: via a study of (1) defenses established to reduce associated pain, unpleasure, distress, or (2) a study of compensations to restore crucial levels of pleasure which had been lost.

This chapter focuses primarily upon compensatory processes aiming to restore critical levels of pleasure among infants who have been deprived of empathic interrelationships as a primary supply line of pleasure. The chapter focuses only secondarily upon the vicissitudes of defenses against pain and distress.[1]

THE COMPENSATORY VALUE OF HYPER AND HYPO STATES AMONG INFANTS DEPRIVED OF EMPATHIC CARE

According to classic learning studies of animal behavior, deprivation of such primary needs as food, water, or warmth activates propulsive states of diffuse hyperactivity usually referred to as "random" behavior. Such propulsive "random" behavior eventually brings the animal in contact with the needed substances serving to satisfy its primary needs. In turn, the maintenance and repetition of those aspects of the random behavior which immediately precede the rewarding condition will tend to be reinforced (Hilgard and Marquis, 1961, pp. 67–68).

Likewise, the following summary draws attention to the compensatory rewarding effects of *HYPER* and *HYPO States* arising from deprivation of empathic care during infancy: (1) a deprived infant's *HYPER States* in the form of excessive agitation and intense vocalization may eventually succeed in mobilizing an adult to attend to the infant's needs and thereby provide a source of pleasure and reward; (2) a deprived infant's *HYPER States* in the form of headbanging, rocking, locomotor or vocal *HYPER*-motility may eventuate in the infant's rudimentary ego supplying itself with much

---

[1]If we assume that there is a reciprocally antithetical relation between pleasure and unpleasure (pain, unlust, or distress) then the compensatory restoration of pleasure indirectly amounts to a defensive protection from unpleasure or distress. For this reason a reference to the difference between compensatory restoration of pleasure and the defensive protection from unpleasure is a matter of emphasis.

needed arousal and tranquilizing emotional stimulation, and thereby provide a source of pleasure and reward; (3) a deprived infant's *HYPER States* in the form of hyperactivity and hypersensitivity may bring the infant into contact with its own erogenous and erotic body surface and bodily products as a much needed source for pleasure and reward reinforcing the maintenance and repetition of such behavior; and (4) a deprived infant's *HYPO States* may eventuate in the partial withdrawal of the infant from the hostile environment; the resulting "hibernation" then may become a primary source for tranquility and thereby provide a source of pleasure and reward derived from internal visceral processes. Subsequently, one or more of these general forms of behavior may become the basis for a new primary supply line of pleasure and reward which may substitute for losses of empathic care from a depriving caregiver, thereby helping to compensate for the infant's chronic deprivation of empathic care and associated chronic loss of pleasure. These conclusions are elucidated by the following observations.

Type A Compensatory Supply Lines of Pleasure: HYPER States of Crying May Become a Source for the Deprived Infant's Gaining Contact, Attention, and Pleasurable Care from an Indifferent Caregiver

HYPER States as a reaction to prolonged losses of pleasure accompanying deprivation of empathic care are regularly discharged via hypervocalization in the form of persistent crying and screaming (see chapter 4). Such excessive reactions, combined with visual and/or auditory and/or tactile contacts with a caregiver, describe a picture of screaming demandingness which often has been observed to activate an indifferent parent to pay attention to the infant and perhaps grudgingly attend to its needs (Provence and Lipton, 1962, pp. 129–130). For example, an infant's hypervocali-

nay force the indifferent parent to change the infant's
or to give it some milk. By acquiescing to the infant's
ids," the parent may gain some hope of obtaining
peace and quiet and a chance to sleep. Additionally, infants'
HYPER States with hypervocalization may serve to supply a
lonely and depressed parent with enough excitement to
rouse the parent's interest in life and to increase the parent's
capacity to attend to the infant's needs (e.g., Wolfenstein,
1955, pp. 381–382, 388). In other cases, an infant's *HYPER
States* with hypervocalization may incur the wrath of a potentially sadistic parent so as to provide the infant with
increased stimulus interaction which at least may help the
infant to be aroused and not to be alone. Such arousing
stimulus contacts involving the infant's and the caregiver's
anger and resentment, a hostile dependency, may sometimes
be preferable to a lack of *any* contacts at all, which would
leave the infant vulnerable to the complete deterioration
characteristic of hospitalism (Spitz, 1945, pp. 53–74). Finally,
the infant's *HYPER States* of behavior with hypervocalization may provide a basis for the infant's emotional contact
with a masochistic parent who can relate only to a human
being whom they feel endlessly disturbs and torments them
(Anthony, 1984, p. 263). Thus, it is not difficult to realize how
an infant's *HYPER* "demandingness" can be reinforced and
rewarded as early as the first months of life, a basis for the
establishment of a hostile dependency, a hyperpiercing crying, and screaming state accompanied by the infant's close
contacts and attachments to the caregiver.

This concept of a rejected infant becoming attached to
its caregiver via screaming, crying, and via resistive behavior
was introduced and investigated by Mary Ainsworth in 1978.
Ainsworth's text, *Patterns of Attachment,* presents her experimental findings pertaining to deprived and rejected infants
establishing such "anxious resistant" and/or "avoidant reac-

tions" (Ainsworth, Blehar, Waters, and Wall, 1978, pp. 350–353).[2]

Type B Compensatory Supply Lines of Pleasure: An Infant's HYPER Turning Away from Contacts with the Depriving Caregiver and Turning Toward Its Own Rudimentary Ego Motor-Manipulation of the Inanimate Environment

If the caregiver's ego fails to provide the infant a source of sufficient pleasure, the infant's own behavior itself may provide a source for arousal, comfort, and pleasure. Thus, the infant's repetitive vocalizations may provide a temporary substitute for parental vocalizations; the infant's own repetitious rocking may become a crude substitute for parental rocking; and the infant's own head-banging may become a crude substitute for vigorous parental play which the infant has never received. Other forms of hypermotility eventually may provide more complex forms of tranquilizing and/or arousal self-stimulation which can become an important compensatory source of pleasure for the infant. By varying its patterns of rhythmic involvement, the infant may crudely supply itself with arousal as well as tranquilizing and comforting sources of stimulation and compensatory pleasure (Greenacre, 1954, pp. 19–20; Escalona, 1963, p. 226).

This same form of adjustment has been noted in relation to experimental studies of monkeys who have been isolated from tactile–kinesthetic contacts with other monkeys during the first six months of life. Such isolated infant

---

[2]Ainsworth's groups A, B, and C babies (pp. 314–316) should not be confused with this chapter's reference to types A, B, and C compensatory supply lines of pleasure.

monkeys "learned to produce their own [tactile] kinesthetic stimulation" (Suomi, 1990, p. 147) by "self-clasping" and "self-orality" behavior (p. 146) and by developing "idiosyncratic patterns of repetitive stereotyped behavior" (pp. 146, 147). Subsequently, they continued to supply themselves with kinesthetic stimulation and to "actively avoid most social contact" (p. 147).

Margaret Mahler has noted that even more subtle sources of sensory self-stimulation are employed by infants and little children: some babies develop the habit of making rhythmic noises or humming; still other children who are learning to talk, repeat words persistently and make rhymes (Mahler, 1968a, p. 102). In this way, a dependence upon their own hyperactive rudimentary ego may provide a new supply line of arousal and tranquilizing stimulation, pleasure, and reward to compensate for loss or deprivation of empathic care.

Furthermore, when the infant's motor capacities mature, and hypermotility in the form of hyperlocomotion is in a position to supplement or replace head-banging, bed-rocking, and rolling as a source for motor discharge, the infant and toddler obtain a source not only for kinesthetic, proprioceptive stimulation but also for new, ever-changing, visual, tactile, olfactory, gustatory, and auditory contacts with the inanimate environment as an abundant source of arousal stimulation. Thus, Greenspan and Lieberman refer to the case of infant "Albert" who seemed to derive "the impetus for continued development more from his exploration of the inanimate environment than from his interactions with his [depriving] mother" (Greenspan and Lieberman, 1989, pp. 554–555). The infant may soon learn that if it cannot control its caregiver as a supply line of pleasure, at least it can control the inanimate world. Thus, it was consistently found that rhesus monkeys reared for at least the first six months of life in tactile isolation "actively avoided [turned away from] most social contact," even subsequently "as adolescents and adults" (Suomi, 1990, pp. 147–149). In turn, similar monkeys turned to the inanimate environment where they were able to become bonded to an inanimate surrogate mother. Suomi points out that "Harlow's [deprived] infant monkeys consistently formed lasting and functionally important attachments to these [inanimate] cloth-covered surrogates (Harlow, 1958, pp. 673–685; Suomi, 1990, pp. 130–131).

Presumably, the more the infant is deprived of empathic care from its caregiver, the more it will learn to turn away from its caregiver or from other human beings,[3] and the more it will depend upon its own compensatory motor manipulatory contacts with the inanimate world, to offer itself essential arousal and comforting–tranquilizing stimulation as sources for pleasure. Such a deprived infant who learns to count upon its contacts with the inanimate environment may grow into a child who treats people as inanimate objects, that is, as something to be controlled and mechanically manipulated (Mahler, 1968a, pp. 64, 101–102, 136). Likewise, a deprived infant gradually may learn to count only upon itself and not upon others, that is, to trust[4] only itself. It is easy to understand how such infants may grow up to feel that only their own "supply-line" is "good," that is, pleasurable, and how they may come to trust and react positively only to themselves and not to trust others (whereby they turn away from others' attempts to help and turn only to their own contrivances). However, the inadequacy of supplies offered by the infant's rudimentary ego, for example, the inadequacy with

---

[3] See Mary Ainsworth's classification, group A: "avoidant" attachments (Ainsworth, Blehar, Waters, and Wall, 1978, p. 316).

[4] An infant's inability to trust refers to the infant's negatively turning away from a caregiver offering help and care. Conversely, an infant's ability to trust refers to positively turning toward the caregiver offering help and care.

which the infant can offer itself pleasurable tranquilizing or arousal forms of stimulation at times of need, leaves the infant still depleted of sufficient care. Escalona concludes that such "precocious organization of the ego may. . . be considered equally as deleterious a development as delayed organization" (Bergman and Escalona, 1949, p. 349).

The following case of Brody and Axelrad's provides an illustration of deprivation of empathic care during infancy as an antecedent for the infant's turning away from human contacts and instead turning toward its own ego motor-manipulation of the inanimate environment.

Case 21: Mrs. F and Baby Frank
(Brody and Axelrad, 1970, pp. 317–330)

Deprivation of Empathic Care During Infancy:
Mrs. F displayed "no affection, no appreciation, no spontaneity" toward Baby Frank (p. 328). Her attentiveness to him was "rote and affectless" (p. 327). She would stroke him mechanically and inattentively (p. 322) "jiggle his body while she fed him and would withdraw her nipple when he was still bent on sucking" (p. 319). "She talked to him now and then but not in response to him" (p. 327). At night Mrs. F would have left him to shriek away crying were it not for her fear of the neighbors complaining. She believed that if he shrieked long enough he would learn to get out of the habit (p. 326).

Turning Away from Human Beings and Toward the Infant's Own Ego Motor-Manipulation of the Inanimate Environment:
Early in infancy, at the age of six weeks, Baby Frank spent hours alone yet he remained "placid and happy" and was still "more interested in people than in things" (p. 321). "His

visual responses to persons were stronger than to test objects" (p. 321). However, by the time Frank was one year old, he deteriorated to the extent that Brody and Axelrad reported:

> [T]he infant is striving to relate to persons but no real joy is visible in his contacts with people. He watches them more than he engages with them. He is more comfortable with inanimate objects... [p. 330].

Type C Compensatory Supply Lines of Pleasure: HYPER Turning Away from Contacts with the Depriving Caregiver and Turning Toward the Infant's Sensory Contacts with Its Own Body Surface, Body Products, and Body Orifices, and to Sensation-Seeking Associated with One or More of the Five Senses

The concept of the infant's own body sensation-seeking is understood to involve erogenous and erotic, tactile, olfactory, gustatory, auditory, and visual stimulation as compensatory sources of pleasure.

If the infant fails to receive sufficient supplies of pleasure and comfort from the parental ego or from its own inadequate ego, the infant may turn toward its own erogenous body anatomy, body functions, and body products. The erogenous–erotic reactions directly associated with stimulation of the lips, navel, genitalia, and anal mucous membranes, as well as sensory contacts with soft, warm, and slippery body products (i.e., urine, feces, saliva, or nasal contents), may provide an important substitute source of pleasurable supplies for infants who have been severely deprived of empathic care.

Anna Freud refers as follows to these compensatory reactions of deprived infants: "When as happens invariably in an institution, gratification derived from the substitute mother relationship falls far short of what the child would normally experience, auto-erotic gratifications loom larger and fill the empty places in the child's instinctual life" (A. Freud and Burlingham, 1944, p. 606). She adds,

> [Thus], there is a good deal that an infant can do to provide mere pleasure for himself by substituting a part of his own body for the absent mother. When there is no breast or bottle offered for sucking, he can suck his thumb; this will not appease his hunger, but it will give rise to pleasurable sensations in the mucous membranes of the mouth. When there is no mother present to fondle the child's body, his own rubbing or scratching activities on the skin, the ears, or any other part of the body surface will stimulate the eroticism of the skin and produce pleasure. Rubbing or pulling of the sex parts will give rise to masturbatory pleasure ... [A. Freud, 1953, p. 18].

These conclusions have been illustrated by Anna Freud's study of three- to twelve-month-old orphans whose parents had been killed in Nazi concentration camps, a study which offered careful observation of children who suffered severely from early deprivation. These children as infants "were handed on from one refuge to another until they arrived individually. . . at the Ward for Motherless Children . . . [where they] were conscientiously cared for and medically supervised" (A. Freud and Dann, 1951, p. 127). Eventually they were raised at the Bulldogs Bank Colony of the Hampstead Nurseries in London under Anna Freud's supervision (p. 128). After reviewing staff observations at the Nurseries, Anna Freud reached the conclusion that these children who had experienced the severest deprivations from early infancy had to rely extensively upon their own bodies to find comfort and reassurance. Erotic gratifications persisted with each child in one form or another (when the children were already three years of age). Thus,

> Ruth ... had the habit of scratching herself rhythmically until she bled, and [or the habit] of smearing herself with blood. One child, Paul, suffered from compulsive masturbation. Peter, Ruth, John and Leah were all inveterate thumbsuckers. Peter and Ruth [sucked] noisily and incessantly during the whole day.... Miriam sucked the tip of her tongue, manipulating it with her teeth until she fell asleep. With Peter, sucking changed ... to "smoking" carried out with match sticks, twigs, grass blades [A. Freud and Dann, 1951, pp. 147–148].

Similar observations have been described by Spitz who found that "fecal games ... appeared frequently [among the deprived infants]. In the case of Aethelberta, for instance, as well as in that of another child, the games consisted in rolling fecal pellets which seemed to be the only toy these children enjoyed. Aethelberta continued the fecal games ... in the form of social games" in which she tried to feed her partner with fecal pellets. In another case, the fecal pellets were used for covering the bed with a layer of feces and for throwing fecal pellets out through the bars of her cot (Spitz and Wolf, 1946, p. 341).

Moloney points out that the children who have received insufficient pleasurable supplies from parental figures will eventually supply pleasurable stimulation to themselves. The little child "sucks himself, fondles his ear, or nose or any part of the body.... He scratches or tickles himself. He wallows in [his] warm feces or urine. He tickles his nose with a [pillow] feather or [blanket] fuzz. The possibilities of playing mother to himself are legion. Once introduced, it is not easy to rob him of these unsuspected substitutes for the delinquent parent" (Moloney, 1949, p. 340).

These observations lead to the conclusion there exists a continuum in the degree to which the infant's own hyperactive contacts may involve its erogenous and erotic body surface and body products as a source of compensatory arousal, tranquility, and pleasure. All infants, to some degree, will fondle their own bodies and play with their body products. However, the greater the degree to which the infant fails to be appropriately rocked, patted, played with, bathed, soothed with baby oil, powdered, and groomed by a parent or parent substitute, and the greater the degree to which the infant is deprived of much needed periods of arousal stimulation, tranquilizing stimulation, and pleasure stimulation, the more rewarding will be the infant's excessive stimulation of its own body and its contacts with its urine and feces.

Type D Compensatory Supply Lines of Pleasure:
An Infant's Turning Away from Physical and Emotional
Contacts with Its Depriving Caregiver and Withdrawal
into HYPO States of Lethargy and Sleep

If stress from deprivation of empathic care during infancy is prolonged beyond a given magnitude and duration of time, hyperactivity as a basis for compensatory attempts to restore a state of reward and pleasure will eventually fail (i.e., will "burn out"). This formulation is in keeping with Selye's observations with respect to the body's reactions to excessive stress (Selye, 1976, p. 6) and, in this respect, Spitz reports a study of thirty-four infants who, after six months with satisfactory caregivers, were removed and placed with unsatisfactory caregivers. These infants showed a clinical picture which was progressive from month to month. The first month showed increased hyperactive demandingness and weepiness. Then during the second month, the infant displayed a tendency to scream, with a loss of weight and an arrest of developmental progress. Finally, in the third month, there occurred a withdrawal in the form of *HYPO* refusal of contact, involving the infant's lying prone with averted face, and a generalized restriction of motility. After the third month infants displayed a rigid facial expression, freezing of tears, retardation, and lethargy (Spitz, 1951, pp. 269–270; Provence and Lipton, 1962, pp. 129–135).

HYPO States of withdrawal may serve as a primary compensatory supply line of protective comforting and provide a basis for the infant turning to its internal visceral world as a supply line of pleasure and tranquility. This form of adjustment to deprivation of empathic care during infancy serves a positive physiological as well as psychological function: *HYPO States* of bodily functions permit a hibernation-type of existence which favors conservation of energy and thereby protects the infant from exhaustion and death (Engle, 1962, p. 95, cited by Emde, Harmon, and Good, 1986, pp. 146–147).

THE INFANT'S TURNING AWAY FROM A DEPRIVING CAREGIVER

Note, types A, B, C, and D compensatory supply lines of pleasure refer to an ever-increasing degree of the infant's turning away from active contacts with people and the world. Thus the type A infant who is hostilely dependent and anxious-resistant alternates between angrily rejecting and positively clinging to its caregiver. Then, the type B infant retreats still further from its caregiver as it turns to its own ego motor-manipulations of the inanimate environment. Then, the type C infant not only turns away from its caregiver but also from the inanimate environment as it turns toward its own body surface and body products. Finally, the type D infant turns from its caregiver and from its own ego–motor contact with the inanimate environment, and from its passive sensory contacts with its body surface as it turns to its inner visceral states of lethargy, sleep, and withdrawal. These conclusions are in keeping with Modell's observations in relation to the schizoid patient who "withdraws into a form of 'self holding' which is, in a sense, an alternative world. This loss of the 'parental holding' has profound consequences: in some patients an endopsychic perception is recorded where, as children, they feel themselves to be floating off the world or falling off unsupported into the cold regions of outer space" (Modell, 1990, p. 107).

Turning Away Emotionally and Freezing of Affect

A frequent accompaniment of prolonged and severe deprivation of empathic care of infants is a rigid facial expression, drying up of tears, an averted face, an expressionless face (Spitz, 1951, p. 270). These changes direct attention to an inhibition of resonance, an inhibition of elementary empathic reactivity to another individual's feelings as an infant's response to extreme deprivation of empathic care.

Such a freezing of affect has also been demonstrated by experimental studies of animals helplessly subjected to constant pain or distress. Seligman demonstrated how dogs who continued to receive painful shocks no matter what they did eventually showed an emotional deficit, and "evidenced little overt emotionality while being shocked"; instead, these animals sat without motion and endured the shock without whimpering (Seligman and Peterson, 1986, pp. 225–226).

On the one hand, freezing of affect involving freezing of

emotional resonance provides a basis for protecting the infant from pain and distress in the sense of Freud's concept of a "protective shield" whereby hyposensitivity protects the infant from excessively unpleasant and distressful stimulation from the outside world (Freud, 1920, p. 27). On the other hand, however, such freezing of the infant's emotional resonance eventuates in a failure of the infant to care about or have feelings for the lives of the caregiver or of other adults, and a failure to react to them as emotional human beings. Without resonant feeling for other human beings, the infant learns to react to humans as though they were inanimate objects to be controlled for the infant's immediate needs. Thus, freezing of affect, and particularly freezing of empathic resonance as a reaction to chronic deprivation of empathic care, not only contributes to a pathological coloration of types A, B, C, and D *HYPER/HYPO* compensatory supply lines of pleasure but, as illustrated in the following case of Sam, interferes with the infant's capacity for empathic resonant interrelationships as a basic supply line of pleasure and protection.

A CLINICAL HISTORY OF AN INFANT DEPRIVED OF EMPATHIC CARE: AN ILLUSTRATION OF SHIFTS FROM ONE COMPENSATORY SUPPLY LINE TO ANOTHER

Case 22: Rochlin's Case of Sam (1953, pp. 288–309)

Sam's mother was very much in love with his father at the time of his birth; and for the first four months of his life Sam did exceedingly well. He was a "vigorous baby who did not cry excessively." His sleep was undisturbed. He was successfully fed at his mother's breast and his growth progressed normally (p. 292).

Deprivation of Empathic Care During Infancy:
Then, when Sam reached the age of four months, his mother learned that the father was unfaithful while he was away on business trips for periods of a month or more (p. 292). During this period the father turned to alcoholism (p. 293). As a consequence of such rejection, Sam's mother became depressed. Her breast-feedings of Sam terminated precipitously and Sam was put on the bottle unattended (p. 292).

To make matters worse, the father, when drunk, would verbally attack and shout at Sam and at Sam's mother (p. 293). On other occasions, the mother would repeatedly disappear in order to search for the philandering father. Guilty because she neglected Sam, the mother would sporadically indulge Sam with lavish care or would leave him with maids who took excellent physical care of him but offered him little else. The inability of the itinerant maids to speak English did not improve matters (pp. 292–293).

HYPER and HYPO States of Arousal and the Emergence of HYPER and HYPO Compensatory Supply Lines of Pleasure: At the age of four years, Sam's most striking attribute was his aimless restlessness (p. 293). Since the age of two years, he would throw things about and would tear wallpaper (p. 291). By this time he had all but given up reaching out to his mother for emotional contact. His capacity to resonate with his mother's feelings of pleasure or distress became frozen: he would climb on her as though she were an inanimate object such as a chair (p. 293). Having lost his mother or any caregiver as even a partially satisfactory supply line of pleasure, it is not surprising that he turned to his body and to his own rudimentary ego activities with inanimate stimulus contacts as compensatory supply lines of pleasure. Thus, "shortly after the [unattended] bottle feedings began when he was about five or six months old, he started to suck his fingers actively. This continued for the rest of the first year" (p. 293), only to be suppressed by his grandmother's unrelenting determination to tie Sam's hands in order to break the habit. During the year that followed, Sam's *HYPER States* were expressed in the form of voracious eating, another form of turning to bodily sensations as a compensatory supply line of pleasure (p. 293). At the same time, he turned to tactile contacts with the inanimate environment. He would rub his cheek on his mother's fur coat for hours (p. 290) and would sit by the hour in a closet while he would rub himself on the fur coat (p. 290). In Rochlin's words, "The human organism cannot be without an object and when loss occurs it can find only partial compensation in itself" (p. 309). He points out the inanimate substitute amounts to an inanimate mother which will not threaten loss (p. 305). In this way, the infant's own hyperactive contacts with and control of the inanimate environment provided a basis whereby Sam's rudimentary motor manipulation of the inanimate environment became a primary compensatory supply line of pleasure and reward for him. Rochlin concluded that Sam's "predominant quality was the necessity of control over every live or inanimate object" (p. 302) where inanimate and animate were not differentiated for him (p. 293).

Extreme Hypowithdrawal to Compensate for Extreme Deprivation of Empathic Care with Deterioration of Compensatory Adjustments: Unfortunately, by the age of four, just prior to his entering therapy, Sam was subjected to an ever-increasing deprivation of empathic care. His mother would "pound the wall" while she thought of Sam as being "a nasty, horrid little boy" (p. 291). She was so angry at him that "she would squeeze too hard in hugging him"; she would put him into a tub of excessively hot water; she "wanted to smash his head in" and was "unable to get near him" (p. 291).

It is not surprising, therefore, that Sam's compensatory drives to restore a state of pleasure and reward deteriorated to the extent that he became dependent upon his own kinesthetic movements and *HYPO States* of withdrawal as sources for tranquilizing stimulation. Rochlin reported that Sam's "staring" (p. 291) and "monotonous, tedious repetition ... became his comfort as he reduced the world around himself to a fixed, lifeless ... system" (p. 301).

NORMAL AND PATHOLOGICAL ASPECTS OF COMPENSATORY SOURCES OF PLEASURE DURING INFANCY

When are supply lines during infancy a sign of "normal" adjustments and when are they pathological? A moment's reflection indicates that all infants display periods of screaming for their mother, periods of gaining pleasure from visual, auditory, and tactile contacts with the inanimate environment, gaining pleasure from contacts with erogenous body parts and products, gaining pleasure from withdrawal into sleep. Furthermore, healthy infants can be observed changing from one supply line of pleasure to another in accordance with their needs and in accordance with any momentary supply line loss to which they may be exposed.

Pathology, with respect to compensatory behavior, is reflected not so much by the presence of a particular supply line of pleasure. Rather, it appears to derive from the *degree* to which the infant *turns away* from the caregiver as it turns predominantly to the inanimate world, its own body, or the state of sleep. It is the unending deprivation leading to the infant's unending turning to its self and away from others as a source of supplies which provides a source for pathology. It is the chronic, endless, insatiable character of the infant's turning away from human contacts and toward its own ego, body parts, or state of sleep which provides for increasingly pathological states of isolation.

In turn, the infant's chronic turning away from human contacts and concomitant emotional withdrawal interferes not only with his or her capacity for empathic resonance but also with positive reactions of trust as supply lines of pleasure. Additionally, chronic turning away from visual and/or auditory contacts with other human beings, of necessity, interferes with learning as a supply line of pleasure. In general, such a chronic predilection for turning away leaves the infant with a deeply established imprint of negativism.

Pathology associated with chronic deprivation of empathic care during infancy presumably would be exacerbated by the instability of the infant's capacity to maintain stable life-essential states of pleasure over prolonged periods of time (Spitz, 1945, p. 59). Since a deprived infant's compensatory drive to supply itself with pleasure never can match an empathic caregiver's means of supplying the infant with pleasure, it becomes understandable that such deprived infants develop feelings of neediness and emptiness of pleasure. In turn, periods of "neediness" and "emptiness" provide a basis for the endless, repetitive, compulsive, addictive character of the infant's compensatory drives to establish stable states of pleasure. Thus, a chronically deprived infant never being able to establish a secure stable state of pleasure necessary for living, will endlessly, insatiably, compulsively, addictively keep repeating its crude compensatory attempts to attain it. Rochlin's little Sam sucked insatiably on his fingers. Then, when this form of compensation was interfered with, Sam turned to eating insatiably. This form of compensation apparently being insufficient to maintain minimal and essential levels of pleasure, Sam turned to stimulating himself with his mother's fur coat. This activity also was characterized by a compulsivity in that he would rub his face with the fur over and over while he would seclude himself in a dark closet for hours at a time. Finally, as deprivation became increasingly ominous, little Sam regressed to increasingly relying upon primitive isolated modes of compensation: he became almost completely detached from the environment, stared out into space, and became compulsively dependent upon his own kinesthetic movements in the form of insatiable rocking, as a last desperate primary source for comfort and pleasure (Rochlin, 1953, pp. 288–309).

Whereas the case of Sam illustrates a fixation of symptoms established during early deprivation of empathic care, other cases reflect regressions to such symptoms among children who often function more normally. The following chapter focuses upon the occurrence of such behavioral regressions interpreted in terms of a trigger theory of emotional reactivation.

CHAPTER 6

A Trigger Theory of Emotional Reactivation

TRANSIENCY VERSUS IRREVERSIBILITY OF PATHOLOGICAL EMOTIONAL REACTIONS AMONG EMOTIONALLY DEPRIVED INFANTS

The psychiatric literature has presented theoretical differences of opinion as to the irreversibility versus the transiency of symptoms accompanying deprivation of empathic care during infancy.

For example, Spitz concluded that infants suffering from hospitalism continued quite irreparably to demonstrate not only inadequate psychic and physical development but also seriously defective resistance to disease.The reduced resistance continued even after the deprived infants were removed to a sunny ward and were attended by three to five nurses who chatted with each other and would take the infants out of their cots (Spitz, 1946, pp. 115–116). Similarly, Bowlby emphasized how deprivation of empathic care among institutionalized infants with consequent withdrawal and freezing of affect may become the basis for permanent pathology later in life in the form of psychopathic, delinquent behavior (Bowlby, 1951, pp. 30, 50).

On the other hand, a number of investigators have reported the antithetical conclusion that deprivation during infancy does not necessarily eventuate in permanent pathology. Thus, Spitz's and Bowlby's "somber" predictions were challenged in 1950 by Beres and Obers (1950, pp. 214, 232); Lewis (1954, pp. xi, 1, 36, 93); the Clarkes (1960, pp. 33, 34, 35); Rutter (1979, pp. 283, 295, 297; 1987, pp. 316, 324, 325); and Flint (1966). For example, Flint found that the ill effects of children's exposures to a depriving institutional environment could be corrected by offering the infants warm, personal care as well as psychotherapy. "The apparent resilience of some children indicated that they might have a capacity to respond to psychological treatment which could ultimately lead to their rehabilitation" (Flint, 1966, p. 6, see also pp. 5, 35, 66–68).

Actually, investigators from both sides of the debate eventually presented equivalent findings. Beres and Obers, who emphasized the reversibility of symptoms associated with early deprivation, and who followed thirty-eight deprived institutional infants as they matured into adulthood, reported 82 percent of the deprived infants developed severe emotional illnesses such as borderline character disorders, psychoses, and delinquent disturbances whereas 18 percent of the deprived infants became satisfactorily adjusted in adulthood (Beres and Obers, 1950, p. 214). On the other hand, Bowlby (who emphasized the irreversibility of symptoms associated with early deprivation) also noted: "The comparative success of many babies... who spent their first half-year in conditions of deprivation makes it virtually certain that for many babies, ... provided they receive good mothering in time, the effects of early damage can be greatly reduced" (Bowlby, 1951, p. 49). Apparently disagreements pertained not to the facts but rather to the interpretations of these facts. Both investigators found that the effects of early deprivation permeated the lives of a majority of the children studied, yet such findings did not contradict the possibility for some adaptation and adjustment as indicated by the finding that 14 to 18 percent of the Beres and Obers infants managed to grow up to be relatively normal.

The fact that some deprived children developed relatively normally indicates that opportunities do remain for the establishment of normal adjustments, especially when these infants are subsequently offered consistent, dependable empathic care and therapeutic intervention. These views have been confirmed more recently by the long-term investigations of Thomas and Chess who conclude that traumatized infants can change. Thomas and Chess conclude that trauma occurring during infancy is of importance in the etiology of behavioral disorders occurring later in life; yet it is not a fixed, inescapable, determinant of such disorders (Thomas and Chess, 1980, pp. 107–109). Likewise, Langmeier and Matejcek, in summarizing their review of the literature, conclude: "The prognosis of deprivational disorders is not hopeless, neither is it highly favorable. Current opinion suggests that severe and long-term deprivation usually produces serious and at least some permanent effects in a child's psychological structure" (Langmeier and Matejcek, 1975, p. 347). At least hope is offered when pathological regressions rather than pathological fixations occur later in the lives of such severely deprived infants.

EMOTIONAL SYMPTOMS ESTABLISHED DURING INFANCY: REGRESSION VERSUS FIXATION

Individuals who have become regressed rather than fixated may function normally a large part of the time. Such a conclusion is illustrated by the case of Anna Freud's "Paul" who initially, as an infant, had been chronically deprived but as a child oscillated back and forth between functioning as (1) a mature child who became "an excellent member of the group, friendly, attentive, and helpful toward children and adults"; and (2) a severely disturbed child who turned completely away from other people while he became preoccupied with compulsively sucking and/or masturbating (a dependence upon type C compensatory supply lines of pleasure). At such times,"the whole environment including the other children, lost their significance for him" (A. Freud and Dann, 1951, p. 148).

A number of other clinical studies have demonstrated in more detail how infants who have developed specific symptoms in response to severe deprivation of empathic care or in response to other traumatic experiences may demonstrate periods during which they become free of such symptoms but then suffer a regression to the symptoms on particular occasions, such as occurred in the following cases of Margaret Ribble's Baby Bob and Margaret Mahler's Stanley.

Case 23: Ribble's Case of Baby Bob (1965, pp. 5-9)

Deprivation of Empathic Care During Infancy:
Shortly after Baby Bob was born, his mother was deserted by his father. At that time, the mother's milk did not agree with Baby Bob whereupon he refused the breast and began to vomit. "[He] was taken to the hospital and the mother did not call to see him. At the end of the month, [his mother] wrote that she had been seriously ill and asked the hospital to keep her infant until further notice." At this point, the infant was left on a crowded ward "and received very little personal attention. The busy nurses had no time to mother him and

play with him as a mother would, by changing his position or making him comfortable at frequent intervals" (pp. 5–6).

Period of Symptom Formation:
Baby Bob's psychosomatic symptoms which developed in response to such neglect included *HYPO States* of inactivity and listlessness (p. 6) and in spite of careful medical attention and skillful feeding, this baby remained for two months at practically the same weight. His skin became "cold and flabby" (p. 6) and he "showed at this time the pallor which... is typical of infants who are not mothered" (p. 7). "His breathing was shallow. . ." and presently "he looked like a seven-month fetus but with a strange appearance of oldness" (p. 6).

Period of Symptomatic Recovery:
Baby Bob did not become fixated to his symptoms once he was nursed back to physical and emotional health by a volunteer mother who was instructed that Baby Bob "needed love more than he needed medicine" (p. 7). Thus, his symptoms seemed to disappear following his volunteer mother's practice of holding Baby Bob warmly, stroking his head gently, singing and speaking softly to him (p. 7).

Periods of Regression:
If Baby Bob did not display a fixation of symptoms which had been precipitated by his initial chronic deprivation of empathic care, yet, subsequently, he kept regressing to his early symptoms whenever there occurred even a mild inattention or a change in routine or an absence of the substitute parent. Following each minimal rejection, Baby Bob once again became inactive, experienced intestinal disturbances, ate very little, and became extremely pale. At such times he

displayed deficient body tone and withdrew from reaching out for social contacts (pp. 8–9).

Case 24: Mahler's Case of Stanley (1968a, pp. 82–109)

Traumatic Experiences During Infancy:
From the age of six months on, Stanley had suffered from an inguinal hernia accompanied by "intense pain which would come on suddenly... [so that] all of a sudden Stanley would break into violent crying" (1968a, pp. 89–90).

Periods of Regression:
At the age of six years, Stanley again would break out crying whenever he was read a story about a baby who cries and was shown a picture of a baby crying in his playpen with his toys strewn outside the playpen (pp. 83–84). Stanley "cried bitterly when he listened to the story yet he often insisted upon hearing it" (p. 83). Margaret Mahler observed that even the spoken word *baby* would switch him on into the "intense and diffusive affective state" similar to that which he experienced when he suffered from intense pain as an infant (p. 87).

A TRIGGER THEORY OF
EMOTIONAL RECORDINGS

The case of Stanley led Margaret Mahler to employ the term *trigger engram* to refer to the process whereby a sensory-affecto-motor engram or recording established during infancy can be triggered by special cues during childhood (1968a, pp. 87, 91). Medically, the term *engram* is applied to the definite and permanent trace left by a stimulus in the protoplasm of a (neural) tissue. In psychology, it is the lasting trace left in the psyche by anything that has been experienced psychically. In the case of Stanley, the reference to a baby crying would serve as a cue to trigger the early sensory-affecto-motor engram or recording of "the sweeping excitation," the traumatic emotion he had experienced during infancy (p. 87).

More recently, both van der Kolk and also Nachman and Stern have proposed in essence such a trigger theory of traumatic emotion according to which an affective traumatic experience can be encoded at the time of the trauma, stored, and then later reactivated. van der Kolk writes:

> Traumatic experiences are encoded in sensorimotor. . . form and therefore cannot be easily translated into the symbolic language necessary for linguistic retrieval. It is plausible that in situations of terror, the experience does not get processed in symbolic/linguistic forms but tends to be organized on a sensorimotor. . . level—as horrific images, visceral sensations or fight/flight reactions. These then can be reactivated by affective [and/or] auditory, or visual cues [van der Kolk, 1987, p. 193].

Likewise, Nachman and Stern have concluded that the sensorimotor affect of traumatic experiences during the first twelve months of life "can be encoded, stored, or recalled [reactivated] during this early period" (1984, p. 96). The concept of sensorimotor instinctual recordings is in keeping with Piaget's concept of sensorimotor intelligence as referred to by Greenspan and Emde. Greenspan points out that Piaget's "sensorimotor period of intelligence is so named because the construction of mental structures and schemes is in no way aided by representations, symbols, or thoughts" (Greenspan, 1979, p. 135). In turn, Emde refers to this "prerepresentational self" in relation to the infant's "affective core" (Emde, 1983, p. 165).

On this basis, the term *recording* will be used to refer to the coding of instinctual–affective processes directly associated with past experiences of sensory-affecto-motor discharge, in contrast to the term *memory* which will be used to refer to the coding of higher cerebral cognitive, often reportable, verbalized, intrinsic thought processes.

In terms of these definitions, then, a trigger theory of emotional symptoms states that the exposure of an infant to early traumatic emotional experiences (such as is afforded by chronic deprivation of empathic care) can result in the establishment of sensory-affecto-motor "emotional–instinctual recordings" of the experiences, for example, recordings of the chemical, neurotransmitter reactions of the limbic system within the instinctual brain. Thereupon, according to the processes of associative learning and redintegration,[1] a future stimulus experience that in some aspect resembles the initial experience will be able to trigger the emotional–instinctual recording. For an elaboration of Hollingworth's concept see Mowrer (1950, p. 296) citing Hollingworth (1928, pp. 80–81). Mowrer refers as follows to redintegration based upon associative learning: "Once a total situation has become connected to a given response, a single significant part of that situation will have a tendency to elicit that response."[2] (Mowrer, 1950, p. 296; Anisman and Sklar, 1979, p. 610; Kolb, 1984, p. 241; Weil, 1989a, pp. 154–156, re the concept of "primary instinctual recordings").

---

[1]Redintegration is a term used by Hollingworth and Mowrer (1928, pp. 80–81).

[2]For example, if a little boy screams with terror when he receives a painful shot of medicine at the hospital from a big doctor in a white coat, then on future occasions the little boy may break out screaming in terror when he simply sees the hospital and/or is confronted there by a big man with a white coat. In this case, exposure to one or two components of the association—the hospital and/or the white coat—will have a tendency to elicit the total response of terror. By conditional learning, or redintegration, the terror scene has become triggered in the presence of the white coat.

In accordance with this concept, triggered pathological recordings with respect to early deprivation of empathic care would be able to be analyzed in terms of:

1. chronic losses of pleasure;
2. *HYPER* and/or *HYPO States* of arousal;
3. overall feelings of deprivation; and
4. driven attempts to turn away physically and/or emotionally from caregivers and to turn predominantly toward the self via types A, B, C, and/or D supply lines of pleasure.

Some effects of such reactions to chronic deprivation of empathic care, recorded during infancy and triggered in adolescence, are considered in the following chapter.

CHAPTER 7

Deprivation of Empathic Care During Infancy: Effects Extending into Adolescence and Young Adulthood

THE ESTABLISHMENT OF COMPENSATORY SUPPLY LINES DURING ADOLESCENCE

This chapter focuses upon the hypothesis that recordings of *HYPER/HYPO States*, chronic pleasure loss, and compensatory supply lines of pleasure recorded during early deprivation of empathic care can be triggered and elaborated during adolescence.

Figures 6–9 suggest some of the adolescent and adult derivatives of the four types of compensatory supply lines of pleasure initially established during infant deprivation in an attempt to restore homeostatic levels of pleasure. The charts describe the opportunity for adolescent elaboration of the basic infantile forms of compensation.

It should be kept in mind that individuals who derive pleasure by turning toward positive resonant interactions with other caring human beings can receive further pleasure from their own ego mastery, their own body sensations, and from withdrawal into sleep. Such balanced supply lines of

109

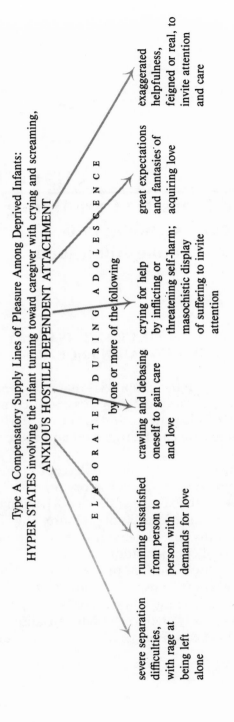

Type A Compensatory Supply Lines of Pleasure Among Deprived Infants: HYPER STATES involving the infant turning toward caregiver with crying and screaming, ANXIOUS HOSTILE DEPENDENT ATTACHMENT

ELABORATED DURING ADOLESCENCE by one or more of the following

severe separation difficulties, with rage at being left alone

running dissatisfied from person to person with demands for love

crawling and debasing oneself to gain care and love

crying for help by inflicting or threatening self-harm; masochistic display of suffering to invite attention

great expectations and fantasies of acquiring love

exaggerated helpfulness, feigned or real, to invite attention and care

Figure 6. Adolescent Elaboration of Type A Compensatory Supply Lines of Pleasure (See Chapter 5)

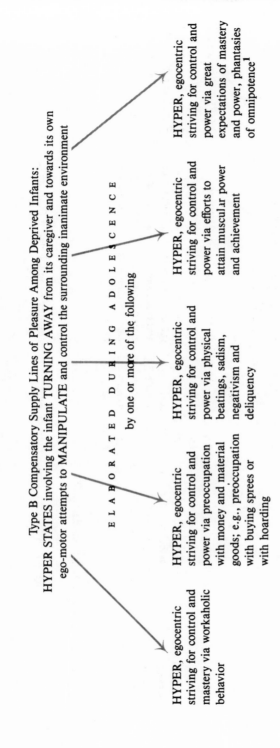

Type B Compensatory Supply Lines of Pleasure Among Deprived Infants:
HYPER STATES involving the infant TURNING AWAY from its caregiver and towards its own ego-motor attempts to MANIPULATE and control the surrounding inanimate environment

E L A B O R A T E D   D U R I N G   A D O L E S C E N C E
by one or more of the following

HYPER, egocentric striving for control and mastery via workaholic behavior

HYPER, egocentric striving for control and power via preoccupation with money and material goods; e.g., preoccupation with buying sprees or with hoarding

HYPER, egocentric striving for control and power via physical beatings, sadism, negativism and deliquency

HYPER, egocentric striving for control and power via efforts to attain muscular power and achievement

HYPER, egocentric striving for control and power via great expectations of mastery and power, phantasies of omnipotence[1]

[1]Modell, 1990, p. 118

Figure 7. Adolescent Elaboration of Type B Compensatory Supply Lines of Pleasure (See Chapter 5)

111

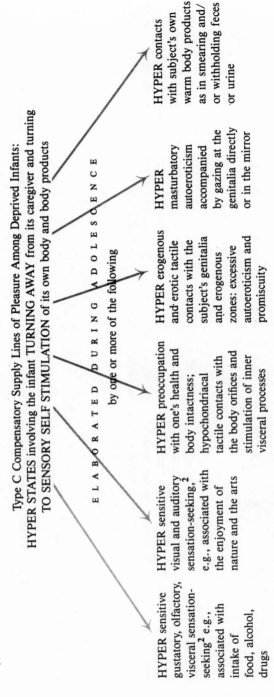

Type C Compensatory Supply Lines of Pleasure Among Deprived Infants:
HYPER STATES involving the infant TURNING AWAY from its caregiver and turning
TO SENSORY SELF STIMULATION of its own body and body products

E L A B O R A T E D   D U R I N G   A D O L E S C E N C E
by one or more of the following

HYPER sensitive gustatory, olfactory, visceral sensation-seeking[2] e.g., associated with intake of food, alcohol, drugs

HYPER sensitive visual and auditory sensation-seeking,[2] e.g., associated with the enjoyment of nature and the arts

HYPER preoccupation with one's health and body intactness; hypochondriacal tactile contacts with the body orifices and stimulation of inner visceral processes

HYPER erogenous and erotic tactile contacts with the subject's genitalia and erogenous zones: excessive autoeroticism and promiscuity

HYPER masturbatory autoeroticism accompanied by gazing at the genitalia directly or in the mirror

HYPER contacts with subject's own warm body products as in smearing and/ or withholding feces or urine

[2] a term introduced by M. Zuckerman (1979)

Figure 8. Adolescent Elaboration of Type C Compensatory Supply Lines of Pleasure (See Chapter 5)

112

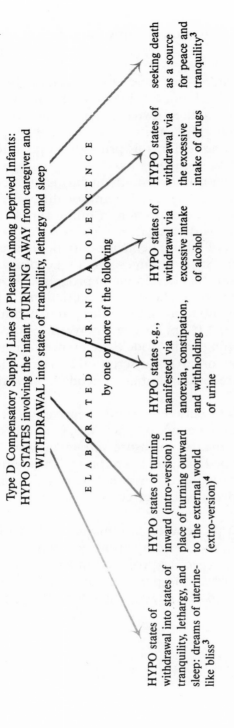

Type D Compensatory Supply Lines of Pleasure Among Deprived Infants:
HYPO STATES involving the infant TURNING AWAY from caregiver and
WITHDRAWAL into states of tranquility, lethargy and sleep

E L A B O R A T E D   D U R I N G   A D O L E S C E N C E
by one or more of the following

HYPO states of
withdrawal into states of
tranquility, lethargy, and
sleep: dreams of uterine-
like bliss[3]

HYPO states of turning
inward (intro-version) in
place of turning outward
to the external world
(extro-version)[4]

HYPO states e.g.,
manifested via
anorexia, constipation,
and withholding
of urine

HYPO states of
withdrawal via
excessive intake
of alcohol

HYPO states of
withdrawal via
the excessive
intake of drugs

seeking death
as a source
for peace and
tranquility[3]

[3]see Freud, S. regarding preoccupations with Nirvana (1920, pp.55-56)
[4]see Jung, C.G., 1921, pp. 427, 452; Fairbairn, 1940, pp. 3,6,7; Mahler, 1968a, p. 16

Figure 9. Adolescent Elaboration of Type D Compensatory Supply Lines of Pleasure (See Chapter 5)

113

pleasure contrast with supply lines of individuals who turn away from other caring human beings and instead turn primarily to themselves: to their own ego mastery and control, and/or to their own bodily sensations, and/or to withdrawal into states of sleep and lethargy as primary supply lines of pleasure, as described in Figures 7–9.

Note that the supply lines prominent during infancy are directly based upon diffuse *HYPER* and/or diffuse *HYPO States*. In turn, note that elaboration of infant supply lines during adolescence, as described in Figures 6, 7, 8, and 9 involves conversion of diffuse behavior into highly specific forms of behavior. Such changes are in keeping with Werner's observations that development progresses from "a state of relative globality and lack of differentiation to a state of increasing differentiation, articulation, and hierarchic integration" (Werner, 1957, p. 126 cited by Wolff, 1960, p. 29). So are they in keeping with Modell's reference to Freud's term *Nachtraglichkeit* or the retranscription and elaboration of a sensorimotor recording initially encoded early in life (Modell, 1990, pp. 2, 3, 18).

The relationships between chronic deprivation of empathic care and the emergence of types A, B, C, and D compensatory supply lines of pleasure *during infancy* have already been described in detail in chapter 5. The summary of these findings in Figures 6, 7, 8, and 9 are based upon the observations of specialists referred to in chapter 5 and Table III.

The relationships between chronic early deprivation and types A, B, C, and D compensatory supply lines of pleasure *during adolescence* as projected in Figures 6–9 are reminiscent of observations presented by Karen Horney over a half-century ago. Horney concluded that the origin of

TABLE III

Specialists whose findings have contributed to an
Understanding of Types A, B, C, and D
Supply Lines of Pleasure during Infancy

type A supply lines	anxious resistant hostile dependent attachments	Mary Ainsworth Ainsworth, Blehar, Waters, Wall (1978, pp. 152, 314-316, 353)
		John Bowlby (1988, pp. 166-167)
type B supply lines	sensorimotor egocentric manipulation of the inanimate world	Paul Bergman and Sybille Escalona (1949, p. 349)
		Gregory Rochlin (1953, pp. 288-309)
type C supply lines	attachments to the body and body products	Anna Freud (1953, p. 18)
		Anna Freud and Dorothy Burlingham (1944, p. 606)
		Anna Freud and Sophie Dann (1951, pp. 147-149)
		René Spitz and Katherine Wolf (1946, p. 341)
		J. C. Moloney (1949, p. 340)
type D supply lines	withdrawal into uterine-like states	Phyllis Greenacre (1945, p. 47)

neurosis invariably lies in "a lack of genuine warmth and affection," during early childhood:

> [A] child can stand a great deal of what often is regarded as traumatic—such as sudden weaning. . . as long as inwardly he [or she] feels wanted and loved. Needless to say, a child feels keenly whether love is genuine, and cannot be fooled by any faked demonstrations. The main reason why a child does not receive enough warmth and affection lies in the parents' incapacity to give it on account of their own neuroses [Horney, 1937, p. 80].

Thereupon, Horney concluded that such deprivation of love and care sets the stage for the following behavioral symptoms[1] (which are equivalent to those listed here under the headings of types A, B, C, and D).

Type A descriptions of adolescent compensatory supply lines of pleasure are in keeping with Horney's observations that a history of early deprivation may provide a basis for anxiety (pp. 80, 92) leading to: (1) "the neurotic need for affection" (Horney, 1937, pp. 96, 102–103); (2) excessive demandingness and possessiveness of human attachments (pp. 129, 140); (3) masochistic wallowing in suffering as a means of inviting sympathy (pp. 141, 144); (4) driven helpfulness and compliance to inveigle others to like them in return (pp. 142, 143). This conclusion was reached at approximately the same time by Lauretta Bender who wrote that "if loving maternal care is interrupted at an early age or is never provided, the personality becomes arrested at the infantile level" and the individual becomes "insatiable in his demands for love and attention" (Bender, 1975, pp. 436–437).

---

[1]According to Horney, the intermediary variable is anxiety (1937, p. 92). For a definition of anxiety and agitation, see Appendix 4.

Type B descriptions of adolescent compensatory supply lines of pleasure are in keeping with Horney's observations that a history of early deprivation may provide a basis for anxiety (pp. 80, 92) leading to the neurotic quest for power, possession, and control (Horney, 1937, pp. 162–163, 166–177).

Type C descriptions of adolescent compensatory supply lines of pleasure are in keeping with Horney's observations that a history of early deprivation may provide a basis for anxiety (pp. 80, 92) leading to the neurotic need for body stimulation in the form of excessive sexuality (Horney, 1937, pp. 52, 147, 153). This same conclusion was presented by Bender (1935, pp. 49–64, cited by Bender, 1975, p. 437).

Type D descriptions of adolescent compensatory supply lines of pleasure are in keeping with Horney's observations that a history of early deprivation may provide a basis for anxiety (Horney, 1937, pp. 80, 92) leading to a dependence upon narcotizing drugs or alcohol (p. 52) and other forms of withdrawal (p. 98).[2]

---

[2]Karen Horney has emphasized the importance of early deprivation of warm, caring, mothering as a source for emotional pathology (1937, p. 80). Likewise, Harry Stack Sullivan has emphasized the detrimental effects upon the self eventuating from a lack of empathy during infancy (Sullivan, 1953, p. 41). Alfred Adler has emphasized the importance of early neglect as a source of pathological self-concept and for reactions of overcompensation (A. Adler, 1956, pp. 370–371).

Only slowly have these contributions of the interpersonal schools of psychoanalysis been incorporated into the matrix of classical psychoanalytic theory until finally today there is a special focus upon the long-term effects of empathic deprivation during infancy. Such progress suggests that there need not be a conflict between the interpersonal and Freudian schools as to which group is "right." Rather, we can seek how contributions from both groups fit together to form a total picture. Furthermore, clinical investigations pertaining to early deprivation of empathic care need not interfere with clinical investigations pertaining to the effects of traumatic sexual instinctual stimulation of children.

DETERMINANTS OF SPECIFIC COMPENSATORY SUPPLY LINES OF PLEASURE DURING ADOLESCENCE AND YOUNG ADULTHOOD

Early Ego Defects

Traumatic exposure to early deprivation occurring at critical stages of cognitive development during infancy can account for lags in ego development. In terms of Freud's concept of reality ego, this would mean that such early deprivation occurring during critical stages of development would be likely to precipitate reality ego defects such as defects in the cognitive control of instinctual discharge, defects in delaying gratification, difficulty in goal-directed behavior in behalf of future gratification, and defects in facing unpleasant reality (Freud, 1911, pp. 219, 220, 221, 222, 223). In terms of the concepts of Piaget and his followers, such early deprivation occurring during critical stages of cognitive development of intelligence would be understood to precipitate cognitive defects involving assimilation, accommodation, discrimination, expectancy, abstract thinking, object permanence, intentional behavior, initiative, motor exploration, and mental exploration of unfamiliar objects and events (Piaget, cited by Wolff, 1960, pp. 40, 66, 84, 104, 124, 146, 176; Greenspan, 1979, pp. 13–14, 301–305, 321, 359; 1989, pp. 1–66; 1992, pp. 5–10). A neuroanatomical and neurophysiolocal background for such functions has been presented by Pribram in relation to his investigations of the posterior discriminatory and the anterior intentional systems of the cerebral neocortex or forebrain (Pribram, 1960, pp. 1340–1344).

    These concepts may help in an understanding as to why a particular compensatory supply line of pleasure may be expressed in a variety of different forms depending upon what stages of cognitive development have been interfered with early in infancy. For example, infants who have suffered severe reality ego damage—severe disturbances of cognitive development as the result of early deprivation—may come to rely upon unrealistic fantasies as a means of realizing types A, B, C, or D supply lines of pleasure during adolescence. For example, he or she may come to rely upon unrealistic fantasies of being loved, unrealistic fantasies of being all powerful, or unrealistic fantasies of possessing sexual prowess as a means of gratification. On the other hand, infants who have suffered less reality ego cognitive damage during early cognitive development would have a better chance of developing healthy reaction formations and sublimations as a basis for gaining love and admiration, mastery and power, or sexual satisfaction as compensatory supply lines of pleasure (see chapter 8, predictions 5 and 6).

Cultural Customs and Mores as Determinants of Specific Compensatory Supply Lines of Pleasure During Adolescence and Young Adulthood

Frequently, behavior established to compensate for states of deprivation during infancy will be triggered during adolescence in essentially the same form as it appeared during infancy; for example, the adolescent with a history of early deprivation may demand love by displaying temper tantrums or may resort to sleeping as a primary pleasure to compensate for triggered losses of pleasure and feelings of deprivation and emptiness, much as he or she reacted during infancy. In other cases, a compensatory supply line whose roots were established during infancy may become highly elaborated and take on new forms, as in the case of an adolescent who uses alcohol or drugs to attain a withdrawn state of pleasant reverie as a compensatory supply line of pleasure. The greater the extent to which compensatory behavior for early deprivation of empathic care is elaborated during adolescence, the greater would be the expected influence of the surrounding cultural milieu in determining the specific forms which such behavior may take. Whether an adolescent turns to alcohol, gambling, drugs, crime, classical music, or religion as a means of establishing supply lines of pleasure and reward to compensate for feelings of deprivation and emptiness, will depend in part upon the cultural patterns of behavior directly or indirectly embraced by family, peers, friends, religious groups, social or community groups. Thus, a culture may be viewed in terms of the types of supply lines it advocates and reinforces. Some cultures will praise the adolescent for drinking; some will praise the adolescent for delinquency and crime; some will preach "live for the moment for tomorrow we die"; other cultures will favor and honor those who attempt to help others and to make a better world with expectations of rewards from an all-loving God and with expectations of kindness prevailing within the world.

Thus, a culture may serve to define the supply lines an individual may be likely to accept as primary sources of pleasure and reward during adolescence and adulthood. However, according to the trigger theory of emotion presented in chapter 6, it is the degree of deprivation of empathic care during infancy which will be the basic factor determining the degree to which the individual will become obsessed with any particular form of compensation adopted (whether it be alcoholic intake or religious experience).

Interruption and Momentary Breakdown of Compensatory Supply Lines During Latency, Adolescence, and Adulthood

Clinical observations suggest that interference with one behavioral mode of compensation is likely to eventuate in its replacement by an alternate mode (for example, see Rochlin, 1965, pp. 126–132). If one supply line is no longer available as a source of pleasure, the subject is likely to turn to another, sometimes more pathological supply line with which he or she had been familiar in the past. Presumably, for each individual, there exists a graded hierarchy of such compensatory measures.

Figure 10 presents an overall outline describing the establishment of the types A, B, C, and D compensatory supply lines. It also describes the effects of interruption of such supply lines. (Solid arrows refer to the processes whereby specific supply lines are established; dashed arrows refer to the processes whereby such supply lines are interrupted). According to the hypotheses presented in Figure 10, the disruption or interruption of a primary compensatory supply line among adolescents who had been deprived of empathic care during infancy may be followed by an oscillation between (1) chronic loss of pleasure accompanied by disorganizing violent *HYPER States* or enervating *HYPO States*; and (2) attempts to resort to a hierarchy of compensatory modes of behavior, often regressed and infantile, one substituting for another as a means of restoring homeostatic levels of pleasure.

The following case vignettes illustrate how even a momentary breakdown of compensatory supply lines of pleasure among adolescents and young adults who had been chronically deprived of empathic care during infancy can reciprocally release chronic losses of pleasure, accompanied by:

1. Disorganizing *HYPER States*, for example, discharged via diffuse agitation or more highly elaborated rage, panic, fear, or violence; and/or

2. Debilitating *HYPO States* discharged via diffuse depression, lethargy, somnolence, or boredom; and/or

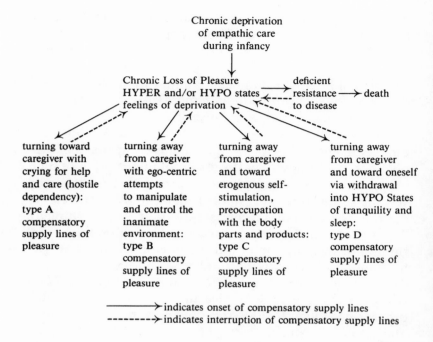

Figure 10. Onset and Interruption of Supply Lines Compensating for Early Deprivation of Empathic Care.

3. A reliance upon a variety of regressive infantile compensatory supply lines of pleasure (see Figure 10).

Case 25: Rubenfine's "Mr. X" (1962, pp. 273–275)

Deprivation of Empathic Care During Infancy:
At the age of six weeks, X was adopted from an orphanage by an adoptive mother who was seldom there with respect to his needs for satisfaction and tension reduction. "A succession

of governesses took care of him throughout his early years during the parents' absences." The adopting mother "was always deeply involved in social activities, charitable, and club work.... She and the [adoptive] father attended innumerable cocktail parties at which she drank to excess. ... On her return from such parties she would be irritable and hostile, and ready to criticize, berate, and physically punish the patient." At times, she would beat the patient with a leather belt (p. 275).

HYPO and HYPER Forms of Compensatory Drives to Restore Pleasure in Adulthood:
When Mr. X was in analysis at the age of twenty-six, even trivial rejections such as a change in appointment time or an unplanned absence triggered feelings of rejection and loss of pleasure, along with debilitating *HYPO States*. After a minor rejection during analysis (interruption of empathic supply lines of pleasure), his usually lively and friendly face became dull and masklike. Then he would sit cramped up and withdrawn (type D supply line) without looking at his therapist, and would speak only in gruntlike monosyllables. He became occupied with his body processes: he sniffed, cleared his throat, coughed, bent over with abdominal cramps, and then would lock himself in the washroom. There, he would turn to his body as he kept blowing his nose for fifteen to twenty minutes (regressive type C compensatory supply lines). At home, he would then avoid human contact and would manipulate the inanimate environment by repeatedly playing the same phrases at the piano for hours at a time (type B compensatory supply lines of pleasure). His interactions centered upon stimulus contacts with "sound but not human sound." Concomitantly, he turned to himself and away from others as he would lose his sexual desires for his girl friend and instead would masturbate many times daily (type C compensatory supply lines). During the initial years

of his treatment this picture was deeply complicated by turning to body sensations through ingesting "huge quantities of alcohol and barbiturates" (type D compensatory supply lines)(pp. 273–274).

Case 26: Blatt's Case of "Helen" (1974, pp. 121–125)

Blatt's "Helen" is another case which illustrates the triggering of *HYPER* and *HYPO States* as well as an alternation of types A, C, and D regressive compensatory supply lines to restore states of pleasure in a young adult who had been severely deprived of empathic care during infancy.

Deprivation of Empathic Care During Infancy:
"After Helen's birth, her mother was confined to bed because of severe back pains and was unable to care for her. The mother was unable to lift or cuddle Helen and the father assumed primary responsibility for her care and feeding." Helen "maintained that she had never seen warmth, love, or tenderness at home" (p. 122).

HYPER States During Infancy:
As an infant, Helen responded hyperreactively and hypersensitively to allergic irritants of the skin and developed infantile eczema (p. 122) like so many of the deprived infants studied by Spitz (1945, p. 59).

HYPER States Reactivated by Minor Losses During Adolescence:
These hypersensitive reactions to irritants were triggered when Helen tried to leave home for camp in her early teens, at which time she developed psoriasis: the hyperreactive skin disturbances were triggered by her immediate loss of contact with her mother (Blatt, 1974, p. 122).

HYPO and HYPER Compensatory Drives to Restore
States of Pleasure During Early Adulthood:
Even temporary losses of love triggered feelings of deprivation and emptiness devoid of pleasure and associated with
HYPER States of tension as well as *HYPO States* of withdrawal into sleep (see Figure 10). Thus, when her analyst was
silent and when she was unable to keep the analyst in sight,
she developed compulsive sleeping (pp. 123–124) (type D
regressive compensatory supply lines of pleasure). "Her
sleep in analysis had a peaceful restful quality" (p. 124). To
quote from Blatt's description: In analysis "she began to
doze. . . . She struggled to stay awake" (p. 123). "Her sleep in
analysis seemed to be in response to the feelings of loneliness
and abandonment she experienced" when she had lost auditory contact with her analyst, i.e., during the analyst's silenc-
es and when she had lost visual contact, i.e., when she was
unable to keep the analyst in sight (p. 124). Such reactions
were triggered by even minor losses of her auditory or visual
contacts with her analyst.

Additionally at times of personal rejection, such as
occurred when her analyst left for summer vacation (interruption of empathic supply lines of pleasure), she frantically
sought pleasure by hyperactively turning from one brief sexual affair to another, each lasting only a few days (pp. 123–
124) (type C compensatory supply lines of pleasure).

Case 27: Weil's Case of Louis (unpublished)

Weil's case of "Louis" illustrates the emergence of *HYPER*
States of rage during the interruption of compensatory supply lines in a preadolescent boy who had been severely deprived of empathic care during infancy (see Figure 10).

Deprivation of Empathic Care During Infancy:
Throughout Louis' infancy his mother would withdraw to
her own bedroom and leave Louis to take care of himself
alone in an empty crib in an empty room.

Infancy: Compensatory Drives to Restore Pleasure:
Louis later recalled putting his arms around himself at the age of two to comfort himself (type C compensatory supply lines of pleasure). He would also play in his crib with his fecal pellets (type C compensatory supply lines of pleasure). Most prominent, however, was his emotional detachment and *HYPO States* of withdrawal (type D compensatory supply lines of pleasure).

Latency: Compensatory Drives to Restore Pleasure:
Louis' withdrawal was repetitively triggered during latency and adolescence. At the age of ten, he adjusted to life by remaining much of the time alone in his empty bedroom where he would eat his meals of bread and cheese. In school, he daydreamed of escaping through the classroom window and balked at doing his schoolwork (type D compensatory supply lines of pleasure).

Although he possessed an extremely high IQ of 160 and later in life became a talented chemist, Louis at age twelve wanted to be friends with no one. Therefore, it became evident that if Louis were ever to emerge from his state of withdrawal and to become emotionally well, he would first need to learn to derive pleasure from someone besides himself. As his therapist, I therefore told him that I would like to give him a small gift each week as a way of helping him begin to learn to receive from others.[3] This effort of mine to help

---

[3]Louis displayed signs of such extreme emptiness during his therapy sessions throughout the first months of treatment that it was decided that it was necessary to take active, unconventional steps in order to help replace his asocial supply lines by supply lines which were more socially oriented. The decision to offer Louis small presents was a first step in the successful treatment of this severely withdrawn child. For other examples, see Buxbaum (1960, p. 249), Weil (1989a, p. 252). Reich (1936, p. 84).

Louis, however, threatened him with interruption of a primary compensatory supply line, his withdrawal (interruption of type D supply lines of pleasure), thereby precipitating a dramatic loss of pleasure accompanied by an explosive *HYPER State* of excitation. Upon hearing the offer of a weekly gift, Louis ran behind a heavy drape hung over the office door and began to scream, ". . . I HATE YOU. . . . I HATE YOU. . . . I HATE YOU," a violent discharge that was at first difficult to fathom. Only gradually did the HYPER outburst of emotion begin to make sense; the promise of a weekly present for Louis threatened to precipitate at least a temporary loss of his all-important compensatory pleasure supply lines of withdrawal. He trusted only his own sources of pleasure and reward. No one was going to interfere in any way with his mode of compensation without calling for a raging battle (see Figure 10).

Louis finally did accept presents from me as his therapist. However, he continued to complain about my efforts to help him emerge from his withdrawal and to reach out to human beings. For example, one day he blurted out, "Now look what you've done! You've made me want to have friends and I haven't got any. Now you've made me unhappy." The emotional pain Louis experienced was extensive, but gradually he did begin to enjoy receiving from his therapist and began making friends, a first step in his uphill course to emotional health. Interestingly enough, each step forward Louis took in interrupting and disrupting his pathological withdrawal as a supply line of pleasure and reward was accompanied by disruptive *HYPER States* of displeasure.

Differences in Reactions to Supply Line Losses Among Adolescents with a History of (1) Empathic Care During Infancy, (2) Deprivation of Empathic Care During Infancy

A history of empathic care and comforting during infancy serves as a basis for recordings of tranquil states of arousal which soothe emotional disturbances triggered at times of losses. In contrast, a history of deprivation of empathic care during infancy serves as a basis for recordings of disorganizing *HYPER States* depleted of pleasure—or debilitating *HYPO States* depleted of pleasure—recordings which can be triggered at times of supply line loss. Therefore, the adolescent who had been exposed to extreme deprivation of empathic care during infancy is in double jeopardy. He or she is not only exposed to the immediate effects of inevitable supply line disruptions and losses during adolescence, but is also exposed to the triggering of disorganizing chaotic *HYPER States* or debilitating *HYPO States* recorded during infancy and involving severe losses of pleasure with feelings of deprivation and emptiness.

This concept leads to the conclusion that *HYPER* and/or *HYPO States* and accompanying losses of pleasure may arise from (1) a simple loss of a present supply line of pleasure and reward; (2) triggering of disturbed reactions recorded during infancy; or (3) the interaction of both "simple," "normal" reactions to current supply line losses *plus* triggered pathological, disturbed reactions recorded during infancy. Adolescents who had experienced a basically pleasurable and tranquil infancy would be expected to react to minor or major current losses by at least some temporary loss of pleasure. However, in such cases, triggering of early recordings of tranquility based upon empathic caregiving would be expected in part to "neutralize" or counteract or attenuate current disturbed feelings of loss via a "holding environment" (Winnicott, 1960a, p. 49; G. Adler, 1985, pp. 220–223). In contrast, adolescents who had been chronically deprived as infants subsequently would be likely to encounter two sources of disturbance in the face of minor or major current losses of pleasure. For among these adolescents, current losses of pleasure would be reinforced and intensified by triggered chaotic feelings of loss and deprivation recorded during infancy.

DEPRIVATION OF EMPATHIC CARE DURING INFANCY AS A SOURCE FOR ADOLESCENT BREAKDOWN

Anna Freud's long-term investigations at the Hampstead Nursery have shed light upon the development of infants who had been deprived of empathic care during infancy and who subsequently were offered corrective experiences of empathic care and psychotherapeutic help. This intensive study of infants who were born within German concentration camps and who were subsequently placed in the Hampstead Nurseries at the age of three to six months, revealed that the infants deprived in the first months of life did gradually respond to the intensive care they received at the Nurseries and became relatively asymptomatic during latency. However, with the onset of adolescence these children, without exception, deteriorated emotionally (A. Freud, 1960, p. 60). See chapter 5 of this monograph for a summary of these findings.

Such clinical findings evoke a question as to why many infants who receive abundant empathic care after an initial period of early emotional deprivation seem to do relatively

well during latency but then "break down" during adolescence. An answer to this question possibly may derive from
the following observations of changes which take place during adolescence.

Instinctual Reawakening During Adolescence

During infancy, when the highest cortex of the cerebral
hemispheres is not yet fully functioning or at best is barely
beginning to function (Teitelbaum, 1967, p. 559; Altman,
1967, pp. 731, 741), the mechanisms of the lower instinctual
brain remain free to discharge emotional behavior without
inhibition from the cerebral cortex: during the first months
of infancy the processes of the instinctual brain predominate
as a basis for the discharge of disturbed emotional reactions
in response to deprivation of empathic care. However, during the preschool years and latency period, when the higher
cerebral functions become increasingly dominant, the triggered, instinctually organized, disturbed behavior of the
deprived infant may become more and more effectively controlled and masked by the higher cerebral functions. As a
result of these cerebral controls instituted during latency, the
child with a history of early deprivation may appear to function relatively normally.

   But then, as the result of hormonal changes taking place
during adolescence, there once again occurs a change in the
balance between the forces of higher cortical and lower
instinctual processes, a change which favors an instinctual
reawakening. In Anna Freud's words: "In . . . the early infantile period [and] at puberty . . . a relatively strong id con-
fronts a relatively weak ego. These are periods in which the id
[the instincts] is vigorous and the ego enfeebled" (A. Freud,
1937, p. 140). This instinctual reawakening accompanying
the hormonal changes of puberty would account for the

exaggerated adolescent reactivation of emotional, instinctual reactions which had been recorded during infancy and which had been granted a relatively dormant position during latency. According to this hypothesis, both normal and pathological emotional, instinctual reactions which had been recorded during infancy would be in a position to be fully reawakened and exposed during adolescence. Infants who had experienced warm, close, and pleasurable contacts with their mother's body would experience during adolescence an intense reawakening of such feelings and an urge to repeat the recorded physical and emotional contacts with other human beings. On the other hand, infants who had experienced deprived, empty experiences would be expected to experience during adolescence an intense reawakening of such deprived, empty feelings. Instinctual feelings of rejection and deprivation would be triggered among these teenagers who had been deprived as infants; so would prolonged instinctual chaotic, disorganizing *HYPER* and debilitating *HYPO States* devoid of pleasure be triggered.

Amplification of Instinctual Reactions
During Adolescence

At the time of sexual maturity, the tender behavior of the little child is converted into the immensely forceful behavior of the sexually mature adolescent; as the result of hormonal changes, the mild behavior of a little infant may become amplified during adolescence to the point that the resultant *HYPER States* may become overwhelming and out of control. In Anna Freud's words: "Aggressive impulses are intensified to the point of complete unruliness, hunger becomes voracity, and naughtiness of the latency period turns into the criminal behavior of adolescence. Oral and anal interests, long submerged, come to the surface again" (A. Freud, 1937, p. 146).

Thus, adolescents who had been chronically deprived of empathic care during infancy will, according to a trigger theory of emotional reactivation, be likely to experience amplification of one or more of the diffuse emotive responses recorded early in infancy:

1. Amplification of chronic *HYPER States*; and/or
2. Amplification of chronic *HYPO States*; and/or
3. Amplification of recorded losses of pleasure with amplified feelings of chronic deprivation in life often described as feelings of "emptiness";
4. Amplification of chronic turning toward one's self and away from emotional contacts with other human beings; and
5. Amplification of frozen resonance with other human beings.[4]

In turn, such *HYPER* or *HYPO States* of chronic loss of pleasure, accompanied by a predilection for turning away from other human beings, will set the stage for one or more of the following problems pertaining to social adjustments, work, and learning:

1. Peers are likely to tend to dislike a self-centered adolescent who turns away from them, who is "empty," and who is either *HYPER* jittery and explosive or *HYPO* and morose. In turn, such peers will tend to turn away and reject such a deprived adolescent.

---

[4]In this way such a deprived adolescent will tend to choose to be alone and to be self-centered even though such tendencies to become self-centered may be partially hidden by patterns of social behavior learned during latency.

2. Schoolwork will also tend to deteriorate when (a) *HYPER States* of excessive arousal flood and disrupt higher cognitive brain processes or when (b) enervating *HYPO States* of arousal do not sufficiently reinforce such cognitive processes (see chapter 4). Additionally, schoolwork will be prone to deteriorate when the deprived adolescent is not supplied with enough pleasure and reward to reinforce the maintenance and repetition of schoolwork. Such an individual will tend to turn to types C and D compensatory supply lines of pleasure in the form of withdrawal into states of lethargy and sleep and/or in the form of erogenous or erotic contacts with their own body or body products. Too often such an adolescent will be likely to stay in bed too long in the morning and to cop out on doing homework in the evening. Furthermore, the adolescent with a history of chronic deprivation during infancy and with triggered recordings of turning away from visual contacts and from auditory contacts often will do poorly in school because of difficulties in paying attention to his or her teacher's lectures.

3. Parents frequently fail to understand such an adolescent. Some parents become impatient, punish and scream at such an adolescent with accusations such as "you no good bum . . . , you good-for-nothing . . . , you don't even try . . . , you won't do your work . . . , you won't even try to get up on time . . . ," or as one mother screamed, "you need a good kick in the ass." Parents often find it difficult to give up hitting such children who defiantly turn away from parental requests and who are frozen with respect to any empathic responsiveness.

In other cases, the rejected individual may pathetically attempt to compensate for feelings of deprivation and emptiness by turning to the land of fantasy with daydreams of glory and of grandeur.

Pathology becomes intensified when a history of deprivation of empathic care is combined with a history of sexual and physical abuse during infancy, childhood, and/or adolescence. Unfortunately, the complexity of symptoms associated with early deprivation are compounded when adult genital erotic stimulations activate night terrors, fugue states, phobic hallucinations (Weil, 1989a, pp. 31–84), and/or when physical beatings activate severe negativism, preoccupation with killing others, or killing oneself (Weil, 1989a, pp. 85–126). Too many families are ridden with all three sources of pathology: deprivation, corporal abuse, and sexual abuse.

Thus, adults are more likely to beat hostile–dependent or anxiously avoidant deprived infants and children who, for example, negatively turn away from hearing parental demands and requests. At the same time, adults are more likely to beat deprived infants and children who are relentlessly *HYPER:* who keep the parents up through the night with crying, screaming, headbanging, or noisy bedrocking, or who talk incessantly, eat too quickly, and insist upon touching and breaking household objects (Steele, 1980, p. 67).

On the other hand, adults are more likely to become sexually involved with deprived infants and children who excessively turn to erotically touching their body parts, including their genitalia, and/or who are hypochondriacally involved with their bodies as primary compensatory supply lines of pleasure.

The Road to Mental Illness

All in all, an adolescent exposed to reawakened and amplified recordings of chronic early deprivation of empathic care is likely to become burdened with one or more of the following exaggerated reactions: exaggerated feelings of emptiness; exaggerated needs to be loved; exaggerated involvement with body parts and body products, urine, feces, and genitalia; exaggerated needs to manipulate and control; exaggerated withdrawal into the land of fantasy; exaggerated rejection by peers; exaggerated failures in learning; excessive punishments and tirades from parents. It is therefore understandable that such an overwhelmed adolescent faces a state of breakdown. It is not surprising to find that leaders from different schools of psychoanalysis have reached this same conclusion. As early as 1937, Horney concluded that early deprivation of genuine warmth and affection is an important source of anxiety neurosis (1937, pp. 79–80). Similarly, Bowlby cited Fairbairn's conclusions that early deprivation is an important source of "schizoid" disorders (see Bowlby, 1988, p. 50). Kohut concluded that childhood deprivation is an important source of "defects in the self" (1977, p. 87). Kernberg concluded that feelings of emptiness and futility stem from severe pathology of object relations during infancy and early childhood (1975, p. 223) and that severe early frustration contributes to the formation of "the borderline personality organization" (p. 28). Winnicott concluded that problems of early mothering provide an important source of "psychosis," "character disorders," and "false self" (1960b, p. 145; 1963c, pp. 256–257).

In considering the etiology of schizoid-type disturbances, Bowlby writes, "There now seems little doubt that when infants and young children are the subjects of insensitive mothering, mixed perhaps with occasions of outright rejection, . . . the effects are deplorable. Such experiences greatly increase a child's . . . despair of ever having a secure and loving relationship with anyone" (Bowlby, 1988, p. 50). "The child and later the adult, become afraid to . . . become attached to anyone for fear of further rejection with all the agony, the anxiety, and the anger to which that would lead" (Bowlby, 1988, p. 55). And Winnicott notes, "The environ-

ment, when good enough, facilitates the maturational process. . . . The reverse process is that of disintegration . . . of the
personality" (Winnicott, 1963a, p. 223). On this basis, Winnicott asserts that in "the treatment of the borderline psychotic patient it is possible for us to reconstruct the dynamics
of infancy and of infantile dependence and the maternal
care that meets [or does not meet] this dependence" (1960a,
p. 55).

In the same vein, Kohut has written:

> I believe . . . that defects in the self occur mainly as the result
> of empathy failures from the side of the [caregiver][5]—due to
> the narcissistic disturbances of the [caregiver]. . . . Even
> serious realistic deprivations (what one might classify as
> "drive" or need frustrations) are not psychologically harmful
> if the psychological environment responds to the child with a
> full range of undistorted empathic responses. . . . The . . . em-
> pathic merger . . . [and] need-satisfying actions performed by
> the [caregiver]—cannot be overestimated: if optimally ex-
> perienced during childhood, it remains one of the pillars of
> mental health throughout life, and in reverse, if the [care-
> giver] of childhood fails, then the resulting psychological
> deficits or distortions will remain a burden that will have to
> be carried throughout life [Kohut, 1977, pp. 87–88].

In turn, Kohut has proposed that disturbances derived
from empathic deprivation require therapy based upon corrective experiences of empathic responsiveness (p. 91).

Finally, Lidz's clinical studies draw attention to schizophrenic pathology arising from interactions between deprived parent and deprived child (1975, pp. 13–16, 31). It is
bad enough if a temporarily unhappy, depressed mother
chronically deprives her offspring during infancy so that the
infant is likely to suffer disturbances pertaining to deficient

---

[5]Kohut uses the term *self-object* rather than *caregiver*.

pleasure during adolescence. But it is worse when the same deprived, empty, unempathic mother may also expose her child to her excessive compensatory behavior throughout her child's infancy, latency, and adolescence. In this case, there can develop an interaction between deprived mother and deprived adolescent, an interaction of two generations within the family in which adolescent and parent both are excessively hostile–dependent, excessively egocentric, excessively controlling, excessively involved with body functions and body products, and/or excessively withdrawn into the land of fantasy. Such a folie à deux interaction within a family can exacerbate already incipient signs of psychotic behavior, especially when the deprived adolescent is not able to become free from such a disturbed entanglement.

Chapter 8 will focus in more detail upon the predicted range of emotional effects which may appear among adolescents and young adults who had been exposed to early deprivation. Evidence will be presented which suggests that (1) compensations for early deprivation are repeatedly characterized by compulsivity and/or addictiveness, and (2) compensations for early deprivation range from pathologically destructive to socially constructive forms.

CHAPTER 8

Predictions

Otto Kernberg has observed that early deprivation provides an important source for feelings of emptiness and depletion which in turn invite addictive behavior. Kernberg draws attention to numerous forms of addictive behavior established among individuals who are plagued by feelings of emptiness: addiction to alcohol, drugs, delinquency, food, and frantic social interactions (Kernberg, 1975, pp. 213–214). Kernberg points out that "chronic experiences of emptiness and futility" are a sign of "severe pathology . . . which stems from infancy and early childhood" (1975, p. 223).

From the neuropharmacological point of view, van der Kolk reaches this same conclusion. "Childhood deprivation seems to predispose a person to a large variety of addictive behaviors including alcohol and nicotine addiction" (van der Kolk, 1987, p. 42). "There is also evidence that social isolation directly affects the number or sensitivity of brain opiate receptors [regulating pleasure], at least during critical stages of development. In one study, social isolation [social deprivation] in young mice was found to cause decreased brain opiate receptor density" (Bonnet, Hiller, and Simon, 1976, p. 338, cited by van der Kolk, 1987, p. 41). A few days of social isolation (social deprivation) cause reduced morphine sensivity in young rats (Panksepp, 1980, p. 111, cited by van der Kolk, 1987, p. 41). On this basis, the affected subject is "more likely to seek the comfort of actions that stimulate the opioid system to cope with" separation (i.e., isolation, deprivation) (van der Kolk, 1987, p. 42).

These conclusions, together with the formulations presented in chapters 5, 6, and 7, suggest that a history of chronic deprivation of empathic care during infancy is accompanied by recordings of chronic losses of pleasure; that is, recordings of emptiness and deprivation involving a depressed opioid system. These recordings would then be in a position to be reactivated and amplified during adolescence. It would be such exaggerated losses of pleasure with feelings of emptiness which subsequently become a source for addictive drives to restore homeostatic levels of pleasure.

This chapter will first focus upon three pathological forms of addictive behavior which, according to hypotheses of Kernberg and of van der Kolk, stem from early deprivation of empathic care and from the associated feelings of insufficient pleasure and emptiness: addictive alcohol intake, addictive sexuality, and addictive therapy-resistant delinquency. The chapter will then turn to two constructive forms of addictive behavior which also may serve as supply lines to compensate for triggered recordings of deprivation, insufficient pleasure, and emptiness: addictive workaholic drives for constructive mastery and addictive altruistic needs to rescue the deprived and oppressed with whom the subject identifies.

PREDICTION 1: ADOLESCENTS WHO HAD BEEN SEVERELY DEPRIVED OF EMPATHIC CARE DURING INFANCY RUN A STATISTICALLY GREATER CHANCE OF MANIFESTING ALCOHOLIC DEPENDENCY AND ADDICTION

Large numbers of people throughout the world have enjoyed the moderate intake of alcoholic beverages on social occasions to elicit a glowing feeling of warmth (associated with dilatation of the cutaneous blood vessels), to arouse an appetite (associated with reflex stimulation of salivary and gastric secretions), and to facilitate social contacts between human beings (Ritchie, 1985, pp. 372–374).

The intake of larger quantities of alcohol has been found to exert an anaesthetic effect upon the prefrontal neocortex, which under normal circumstances inhibits the unrestrained discharge of the instinctual brain core. Alcohol therefore has been consumed to offer an anaesthetic release from higher cortical inhibitions so as to "loosen up" socially restricted individuals (Ritchie, 1985, pp. 372–373). In this connection, alcohol has also been imbibed to facilitate a central nervous system release of sexual restraints (p. 376).

Finally, still greater amounts of alcohol intake, to a greater or lesser extent, can serve the purpose of withdrawal from an unpleasurable external environment of distress into a state of sleep and lethargy during which pleasure is primarily derived from the subject turning to himself or herself, away from others, and to warm, comforting, internal visceral experiences.

The predicted emergence of alcoholism among adolescents who had been severely deprived during infancy becomes understandable in the light of these effects of alcohol intake upon the central nervous system functions. Excessive alcohol intake provides a high-powered supply line to compensate for triggered diffuse feelings and expectations of early deprivation; in such cases alcohol intake can serve as a primary supply line compensating for triggered empty feelings of insufficient pleasure:

By pressing the pleasure button[1] of inner feelings of warmth, alcohol can momentarily mitigate deprived feelings of being cold. In this regard, Ritchie points out that alcohol ingestion produces "a feeling of warmth because it enhances cutaneous and gastric blood flow" (Ritchie, 1985, p. 374).

By pressing the pleasure button of social relaxation, alcohol can momentarily mitigate deprived *HYPER* feelings of loneliness and inadequacy, i.e., by releasing the instinctual brain centers from the inhibitory control of the higher cerebral functions. Increasing intake of alcohol frequently eventuates in a state during which "confidence abounds, the personality becomes expansive and vivacious, and speech may become eloquent and occasionally brilliant" (p. 373).

By pressing the pleasure button involved with sexual desire, alcohol intake can momentarily compensate for *HYPO States* of boredom and for loss of pleasure associated with recordings of early deprivation (p. 376).

By pressing the pleasure button of emotional withdrawal from the real world, alcohol intake can momentarily enhance the subject's escape from an unpleasant real world of rejection (p. 372).

Figure 11 suggests how a chronic depletion of pleasure recorded during infancy and triggered and amplified during

---

[1]With respect to the term *pleasure button* as a function of upper limbic-hypothalamic-reticular system circuits, see Heath, 1964, pp. 224, 226, 228–229, 233, 235.

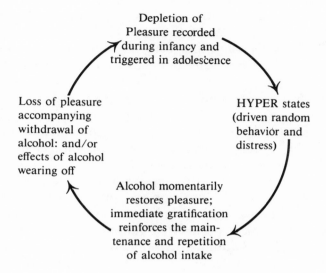

Figure 11. Addictive alcoholism in relation to early deprivation of empathic care.

adolescence can contribute to the onset of alcoholic addiction.

In general, the greater the extensiveness of pleasure-deprivation recorded during infancy, the greater would be the expected need for high-powered compensatory supply lines of pleasure such as alcohol and drug intake to counter triggered expectations and feelings of emptiness[2] during ad-

---

[2]It would seem that a proclivity for addiction would also vary with the degree of pleasure that is derived from substance abuse. For example, the degree of instant pleasure and reward derived from heroin is so extreme that most any individual can become addicted following heroin intake on

olescence. Whether an emotionally deprived infant grows up to drink excessively or to take drugs, according to Vaillant, also will be determined by the cultural patterns associated with the subject's home and peer group and the customs and mores predominating in his or her own community and subculture (Vaillant, 1983, pp. 59–63). A group which favors drinking offers its members feelings of recognition, attention, belonging, and praise. Thus, in conjunction with the intake of alcohol, the mirror-support of group members provides an important source of pleasure compensating for early feelings of emotional deprivation.

These hypotheses pertaining to addictive alcohol intake during adolescence as a function of deprivation of empathic care during infancy should be able to be further investigated via a clinical project, paralleling Vaillant's forty-year investigation. Whereas Vaillant's investigation focused upon alcoholism as a function of maladjustment taking place during childhood and adolescence (as reported during young adulthood) (Vaillant, 1983, pp. 239–278, 311, 322–323), the investigation being proposed herein focuses upon alcohol addiction as a function of emotional deprivation of empathic care measured directly and operationally during infancy. This proposed study might be carried out in a long-term project similar to that of Egeland and Erickson at the University of Minnesota, begun in 1975, as a basis for tracing the development of physically and emotionally neglected infants (Ege-

---

repeated occasions. In contrast, individuals may become addicted to alcohol and to overeating even though not all people who regularly eat food or imbibe alcohol become addicted overeaters or addicted alcoholics. However, individuals who need to press pleasure buttons over and over again to compensate for triggered states of pleasure-loss, feelings of deprivation, and emptiness do become easy candidates for becoming addicted to any constant repetitive source of instant pleasure whether it involves the intake of food, alcohol, or drugs. In some cases, addicts easily become poly-drug abusers.

land, 1985, p. 1; Egeland and Erickson, 1987, p. 116; Erickson and Egeland, 1987, p. 157).

PREDICTION 2: ADOLESCENTS WHO HAD BEEN SEVERELY DEPRIVED DURING INFANCY RUN A STATISTICALLY GREATER CHANCE OF MANIFESTING SEXUAL DISTURBANCES INCLUDING SEXUAL ADDICTIONS

Harlow and Harlow concluded from their experimental studies that (1) monkeys raised in separate isolated cages each containing an inanimate surrogate mother and (2) "monkeys raised in [separate] bare wire cages with no source of contact-comfort other than a gauze diaper pad . . . without question [became] socially and sexually aberrant" during sexual maturity (Harlow, 1962, p. 7; Harlow and Harlow, 1962, pp. 141–142; Suomi, 1990, pp. 149–150).

Such findings established among primates lead to the question as to what sexual disturbances arise among humans who have been chronically deprived during infancy. It is possible that deprivation of empathic care during infancy can provide an antecedent for sexual maladjustments during adolescence on the basis of one or more of the following processes:

Retarded Sexual Development

When extreme deprivation of empathic care during infancy depresses the functions of the pituitary gland regulating the development of growth and sexual maturity, a consequent "failure to thrive" and a retardation of sexual development leaves the adolescent devoid of sexual drive, devoid of interest in the opposite sex, and devoid of any development of his or her body's secondary sexual characteristics (Gardner, 1980, p. 378; Money, 1980, p. 373; Money and Wolff, 1980, p. 406). At the age of sixteen one such adolescent patient treated at Johns Hopkins by John Money had grown no taller than a boy of eight years. Furthermore, this boy showed no sign of puberty until the age of eighteen years seven months, and at the age of twenty-one, he seemed to be "socially retarded in romantic and erotic maturation" (Money, 1980, pp. 367–368, 373).

Depressive Withdrawal

When deprivation of empathic care during infancy pre-cipitates prolonged *HYPO States* devoid of pleasure charac-teristic of depression and withdrawal, the triggering and amplification of such *HYPO States* during adolescence would be likely to interfere directly with the adolescent's active expression of sexuality.

Impersonal Indiscriminating Heterosexuality

Infants who have experienced a chronic deprivation of em-pathic care and who therefore have established only fleeting interpersonal contacts with a caregiver will be prone to become adolescents and adults who will display such fleet-ing interpersonal attachments in their sexual behavior. The Don Juan complex illustrates such a predicted outcome of early deprivation of empathic care: the child may grow into maturity with a socialized wish for heterosexual activity but never finds a partner who awakens enduring feelings of pleasure and attachment to warrant some permanency in his sexual attachments. If Don Juan had been forced to abandon efforts to become attached to an adult during his infancy and forced to freeze resonant feelings of empathy during his infancy, then according to a trigger theory of emotional reactivation, it would be expected for this infant to grow up to be an adult who constantly abandons his or her objects of attachment and who displays little evidence of emotional resonant empathy for other human beings (with respect to Don Juan's lack of attachment, see Rochlin, 1965, p. 148).

This conclusion is in accord with Langmeier's summary of the psychological literature regarding infants abandoned within the wilderness: during adulthood these individuals display sexual behavior that is "either autoerotic or uncontrolled and undiscriminating" (Langmeier and Matejcek, 1975, p. 44). "Relationships are unstable and undifferentiated" (p. 44).

In general, when a driven need for orgasm devoid of human attachment becomes a primary supply line or "pleasure button" to compensate for triggered feelings of deprivation devoid of pleasure, the stage becomes set for all forms of promiscuous sexuality (e.g., Don Juan complex, nymphomania, and promiscuous forms of homosexuality). Such driven sexual behavior has recently been investigated in relation to its addictiveness. In 1984, Daniel Goleman of the *New York Times,* in referring to the investigations of Carnes, summed up prevalent findings:

> Some types of excessive sexual activity have all the hallmarks of an addiction and can be treated in a fashion similar to other addictions such as alcoholism and gambling, a growing number of sex therapists believe. People with this problem, who are now being called "sexual addicts" typically use sex as a psychological narcotic [compensatory pleasure button]. They are driven to find relief through sex from feelings of agitation and worthlessness. But once the sexual high ends, they are again overwhelmed by these same feelings and once again feel driven to sex [Goleman, 1984, p. C1, citing Carnes, 1983, pp. 9-61; also see Lidz, Lidz, and Rubenstein,

1976, pp. 340–341; for a summary of the literature involving addictive sexual behavior see Orford, 1985, pp. 91–106].

Narcissistic Autoeroticism

Still other forms of sexual disturbances are predicted to appear in the lives of adolescents who as infants had been severely deprived of empathic care and who, in particular, had been deprived of tactile contacts with a human caregiver. By turning to its own body as a source of pleasure to compensate for a deficiency of physical contacts with other human beings, an infant may become excessively involved with autoerotic contacts as a primary source of pleasure, arousal, and comfort. Thus, with a deficiency of pleasurable tactile contacts between infant and caregiver, the infant's tactile *bonding* may become more markedly involved with its own body or body products or inanimate objects rather than with the body of another human being. According to this proposition, during infancy the stage is set for the triggering of similar physical attachments later in life, especially at the time of instinctual reawakening during adolescence. If an infant's tactile erogenous attachments are primarily associated with a human being, then the infant will become an adolescent who will become socially and sexually attached to another human being. On the other hand, if the infant's erotic attachments are primarily associated with its own body and body products, the infant will become an adolescent who is primarily erotically attached to his or her own body and body products. Normally the adolescent sexual forepleasure reactions recapitulate the infant's gazing at, touching, and mouthing associated with the mother's warm body. But for physically isolated infants who have turned primarily to their own bodies as a source for erogenous pleasure, it is proposed, the sexual forepleasure recordings triggered during adolescence will be directed toward wishes to gaze at, touch, and mouth their own body parts and body products, a basis for narcissistic sexual preoccupations. A neuropharmacological basis for such powerful pleasure attachments and bonding to the self during infancy would occur via the processes of the inner limbic core of the brain involving opiate-rich receptor areas which regulate reward (and therefore pleasure) (Lewis, Mishkin, and Bragin, 1981, p. 1168; van der Kolk, 1987, p. 41).[3]

Impersonal, Indiscriminating Homosexuality

Addictive impersonal homosexuality is a predicted effect of a specific form of early deprivation, a deprivation of tactile-kinesthetic human contacts with the infant's body. Adolescents (or adults) who had been left to turn to their own bodies and who had become bonded to their own bodies as a primary compensation for deprivation of empathic care during infancy, become vulnerable with respect to becoming involved with homosexual–erotic, mirror forms of sexuality. Consider, for example, the case of an infant male who primarily turns erotically to his own body parts as a compensation for a failure of his parents to pick him up and hold him. According to a trigger theory of activation, at the time of adolescence such an individual will again be likely to turn erotically to his own body and body products and become increasingly involved in discharging upon his own body sex-

---

[3]The infant may also attempt to compensate for a deficiency of tactile contacts with other human beings by relating to them via hypersensitive visual and/or auditory contacts (much as blind individuals find themselves relating via other sensory modalities).

ual forepleasure reactions of looking and touching. For example, such an adolescent may become involved in self-centered masturbation while gazing at his exposed penis directly and/or gazing at it in the mirror, activities which eventually are prone to terminate in orgasm. A related example is presented by Annie Reich (1960, p. 223) and by Zavitzianos (1990, p. 247). In such a case, the adolescent's visual perception of his exposed penis, paired with states of masturbatory sexual excitation and orgasm, provides a basis for emotional conditioning whereby in the future the sight of other penises, "part objects," can gradually activate states of sexual excitation; that is, by the process of stimulus generalization, perception of another individual's exposed penis will be in a position to trigger states of sexual excitation initially associated with the subject's masturbatory mirror gazing.

This formulation leads to the prediction that a male infant who has turned primarily to his own body as a source of pleasure to compensate for deprivation of tactile physical contacts with other human beings will run a greater risk of growing up to become an adolescent who becomes sexually involved with his own penis and a similar penis of another man. Surface mirrorlike sexuality then becomes a source of orgastic pleasure which in turn can serve as a compensation for triggered feelings of deprivation and emptiness. Such types of homosexual reactions have been clinically characterized by a driven addictive urge to go from one body to another, a lack of interpersonal involvement, a lack of lasting attachments, feelings of loneliness, and fears of emotional intimacy (Blumstein and Schwartz, 1983, p. 295; Quadland, 1987, pp. 288–289; Quadland's interview with *Newsweek*, 1984, p. 51). Such reactions of addictiveness and lack of lasting attachments are typical of individuals who have been deprived of empathic care during infancy and who have deeply imprinted recordings of deprived feelings.[4]

Sexual Fetishism

There arises the question as to whether a deprived infant's withdrawal from human attachments and such an infant's substitute bonding with erogenous inanimate objects, for example, with a rubber sheet wet with urine or feces, would provide a basis for triggering intimate erotic feelings toward similar inanimate objects during adolescence. This is to suggest that deprivation of human tactile contacts and of empathic care during infancy may possibly provide one of a number of factors involved in the etiology of impersonal sexual fetishism emerging during adolescence (Greenacre, 1953, p. 90; Spiegel, 1967, pp. 409–410). Significantly, Greenacre refers to fetishism as equivalent to drug habituation, i.e., *addiction,* a term which characterizes all of the symptoms being reviewed in this section in relation to deprivation of empathic care during infancy (1953, p. 79; see also Escalona, 1954, p. 46).

In any case the relation between (1) an infant's deprivation of empathic care with a deficiency of tactile–kinesthetic

---

[4]It is of interest that the female equivalent of such promiscuous male homosexuality appears to be nymphomania, a heterosexual activity. According to Kinsey's studies of 8000 women, driven indiscriminate activites involving hundreds of sexual contacts is not characteristic of female homosexuality (Kinsey, Martin, Pomeroy, and Gebhard, 1953, pp. 474, 475, 476). Perhaps there is less chance for the female mirror gazer to associate (1) the visual gazing at her genitalia and (2) masturbatory orgasm. In such a case, the *vision* of other women's genitalia would be less likely to trigger recordings of masturbatory orgastic excitement.

erogenous contacts from its caregiver, and (2) the emergence of addictive sexual problems, hetero- or homosexual, during adolescence and young adulthood should be able to be tested not only by means of collective clinical evaluations but also by long-term controlled studies.

PREDICTION 3: ADOLESCENTS WHO HAD BEEN SEVERELY DEPRIVED OF EMPATHIC CARE DURING INFANCY RUN A STATISTICALLY GREATER CHANCE OF MANIFESTING ADDICTIVE DELINQUENCY

A number of factors come to mind as instrumental in the formation of delinquent symptoms. The cultural, peer, and family customs and mores are a primary determining factor. If the children are rewarded by parents for delinquent acts, and if they gain the approval of peers for delinquent acts, delinquency will be more likely to be adopted as a supply line of pleasure. If children are born into organized crime and learn delinquency as a way of gaining pleasure, and/or if they learn to identify with a delinquent father who has been irresponsible to family or friends or society, delinquency can be learned as a way of life much as a language is learned. This way of life is reinforced when parents fail to offer children consistent, helpful, and empathic controls of delinquent behavior (Steele, 1986, pp. 288–289).

Another factor related to the occurrence of delinquency is an onslaught of abusive beatings during infancy and childhood (Weil, 1989a, pp. 105–109; 1989b, pp. 190–219). Presumably severe beatings prime so much hate and antagonism toward caregivers that the activated hate and defiance become discharged indiscriminately upon other human beings. The child, in the active role, acts out upon others the harm which he or she helplessly experienced as the passive recipient of cruel punishments from parents (Freud, 1920, p. 17; A. Freud, 1937, p. 113). Clinical cases observed by Weil suggest that the earlier in life sadistic beatings are experienced, the more diffuse and exaggerated and deeply ingrained becomes the destructively delinquent behavior which subsequently appears in the individual's life (Weil, 1989b, pp. 202–212).

Additionally, an even more widespread early contribution to the establishment of symptoms which can be recognized as forming the first steps in the direction of addictive delinquency derives from chronic deprivation of empathic care during infancy. Among these symptoms are an "emptiness of pleasure"; a compensatory "greed for pleasure"; a need to "manipulate the environment"; "frozen empathy"; and "a readiness to turn away from human care." When recordings of such symptoms associated with chronic deprivation of empathic care during infancy are triggered later in life, there occurs an opportunity for several prodelinquency forces to reinforce one another. For example, if an adolescent with a history of early deprivation of empathic care is emotionally cold, is greedy for pleasure, and is ready to treat others as inanimate, then a possible compensatory supply line for restoring states of pleasure is offered by the lure of stealing material goods. Unfortunately, if such an individual is empathically frozen and cold, then making others unhappy by stealing will elicit little resonant distress or concern (Bender, 1935, cited by Bender, 1975, pp. 436–437; Bowlby, 1951, pp. 30–31). In this regard, Sroufe refers to "negative empathy" among delinquent children. Sroufe writes of one behavioral example illustrating the exquisite reversal of affect and negative empathy of some of these children. When one child, NT, complained of a stomachache, then LJ, a delinquent child, smiled and poked her in the stomach. NT cried in pain and said "That hurts," whereupon LJ smiled and poked her again (Sroufe, 1989, p. 90).

Such individuals find it easy to identify with groups of people whose compensatory supply lines of pleasure involve feelings of ego power, mastery, and control by means of hurting, attacking, destroying, and killing other human beings.

In any case, once delinquency is selected as a compensatory supply line to restore states of pleasure among individuals who had been chronically deprived of empathic care during infancy, then an addictive aspect of the delinquency, like the addictive aspects of alcoholism or of compulsive sexuality, can be understood in terms of the driven need to keep pressing "pleasure buttons" to compensate for triggered recordings of chronic deprivation and emptiness. In this sense, the psychology of the addictive delinquent is comparable to that of the individual who indulges in shopping binges, borrowing binges, and gambling binges as attempts to compensate for triggered recordings of chronic deprivation and emptiness by means of plans and great expectations of amassing material goods. In the words of Brandt Steele:

> [These children] have a persistent insatiable longing to find something which will alleviate their tragic ... hunger for love and being cared for. ... What we call delinquency can be used to try to solve these problems albeit in an antisocial way. ... In taking adequate histories of inmates of a state penitentiary [it was found that] nearly every inmate was a victim of significant neglect and physical abuse as a child [Steele, 1986, p. 288].

The addictive quality of delinquent behavior associated with a history of early deprivation is suggested by the common observation that for a large number of such deprived individuals, institutionalization and/or psychotherapy fail to correct delinquent symptoms. A large proportion of delinquents and criminals are not amenable to therapy (McCord, 1978, pp. 284–289; Severy and Whitaker, 1982, pp. 760, 766–

768; Velasquez and Lyle, 1985, pp. 146, 153) just as most addictions are not amenable to individual therapy.

PREDICTION 4: ADOLESCENTS WHO HAD BEEN SEVERELY DEPRIVED OF EMPATHIC CARE DURING INFANCY RUN A STATISTICALLY GREATER CHANCE OF MANIFESTING ADDICTIVE STRIVINGS FOR CONSTRUCTIVE MASTERY

Constructive Mastery in the Lives of Individuals Who Had Been Deprived of Empathic Care During Infancy

Defective ego development has been observed to accompany and follow chronic deprivation of empathic care during infancy. Spitz, for example, measured and recorded severe losses in the developmental quotients of infants who had been chronically deprived during the first year of life (1945, p. 69). If such is the case, how can a deprived infant with a fragmented, rudimentary ego attain mastery and creativity as a compensatory supply line of pleasure? How can poorly developed "deprivational" ego fragments become integrated sufficiently to permit the establishment of ego mastery as a compensatory supply line of pleasure?

Such an advance of ego development would appear to depend upon:

1. The degree of deprivation during the first year of life. The less the degree of deprivation during the first year of life, the greater the chance that a mature ego can eventually develop.
2. The degree of empathic care, constructive help, and guidance the infant receives subsequent to the first year of chronic deprivation. The more appropriate the empathic

care, help, and guidance the child receives subsequent to the first year of life, the greater would be the possibility of corrective ego growth serving the development of ego mastery.

The psychoanalytic concept of reaction formation may contribute to the understanding of ego changes occurring among children who as infants had been deprived of empathic care but who thereafter were exposed to empathic care, guidance, and help. Reaction formations have been described as a superimposed psychological attitude diametrically opposed to an underlying pathological instinctual pattern of behavior (Schafer, 1954, pp. 345–349). See Laplanche and Pontalis (1973, pp. 376–378) for a summary of references to reaction formation.

According to Margaret Mahler, repressions of the discharge of asocial instinctual reactions, that is, suppressions or reaction formations, appear as early as the age of fifteen months (Mahler, 1968b, pp. 15–16). This is also the age when the infant's developmental capacity for goals, plans, and intentions mature (Sander, 1975, pp. 140–143). It has long been recognized that such goals, plans, and intentions are mediated by the prefrontal lobes within the highest levels of the cerebral cortex (Pribram, 1960, p. 1340; Luria and Homskaya, 1964, p. 355; Luria, 1966, p. 156). In particular, prefrontal lobe functions mediate plans, goals, and intentions which inhibit and counter ongoing reactions of the lower instinctual brain (Brutkowski, 1964, pp. 261–262). For example, prefrontal lobe functions have been demonstrated to replace instinctual impulsivity by a capacity for delayed response. Just as prefrontal lobe functions of the neocortex (cognitive goals, plans, intentions) are superimposed upon the processes of the instinctual brain to inhibit, restrict, and counter the instinctual brain reactions, so reaction formation goals can be superimposed upon instinctual behavior and thereby inhibit, restrict, and counter such behavior.

These clinical and experimental findings lead to the hypothesis that reaction formations involve the establishment of prefrontal lobe plans, goals, and intentions superimposed upon the lower instinctual core of the brain. Such prefrontal lobe plans, goals, and intentions, involving learning taking place within cerebral cognitive levels of the brain, can inhibit and run counter to the discharge of underlying impulsivity established within the lower instinctual brain and thereby contribute to the development of effective mastery.

In the case of infants deprived of empathic care, diametrically opposing constructive, socially oriented reaction formations would serve to help counter underlying asocial and pathologically immature reactions. For example, by the process of superimposed reaction formations, the subject counters chaos with perfectionistic order; counters asocial behavior with generosity; or counters attachments to excrement with perfect cleanliness. In particular, with respect to mastery and control, reaction formations may be understood to superimpose at least a semblance of ego mastery upon underlying unintegrated ego fragments in the following ways:

1. Where the chronically deprived infant is likely to respond via *HYPER*, chaotic, disorganized, disintegrated, fragmentary states of disorder, reaction formations operate to counter such reactions and help the child superimpose diametrically opposing efforts to establish states of restriction and order[5] (Schafer, 1954, pp. 345, 347–349).

---

[5] The rewarding effects of such counterefforts to achieve orderliness become understandable when it is realized that reality-oriented perception and goal behavior depend upon temporal and spatial order. For example, if the total thousands of words contained in a textbook are scrambled until they have lost all initial semblance of order, these fragmentary words lose almost all organized meaning. Order is required for meaningful organization and integration of perception.

2. Where the chronically deprived infant has adapted by responding via *HYPER States* of turning away from positive human contacts and from complex positive contacts with the inanimate environment, reaction formations operate to subsequently help the child to superimpose diametrically opposing efforts to turn toward the reality world and to maintain positive contacts with human beings and with the inanimate environment.

3. Where the chronically deprived infant grows up seeking immediate gratification and immediate fulfillment of goals to compensate for emptiness, reaction formations would subsequently help the child to superimpose diametrically opposing efforts to seek delayed gratification and delayed goal fulfillment. Such a process amounts to a superimposed restriction of impulsivity as a means of controlling underlying instinctual impulses.[6]

The following case history illustrates the slow process whereby a deprived infant's reaction formations eventually become superimposed upon weakly integrated ego-fragments to provide a basis for integrated mastery as a compensatory supply line of pleasure.

Case 28: Weil's Case of Paul (Unpublished)

Early Deprivation of Empathic Care:
During his first year of life, Paul was left in the hands of a nurse while his mother wavered between life and death in a nearby hospital where she was being treated for peritonitis. Unfortunately, the nurse believed in "protecting" the infant

---

[6]Anna Freud refers to this form of restriction as an "inhibition ... defending ... against the translation into action of some prohibited instinctual impulse" (1937, p. 101).

from bacterial infections by avoiding physical contacts with him and by refusing to pick him up for play or for feedings. Paul became *HYPER* and spent most of his nights screaming his lungs out, split his lip wide open, and attempted to sleep during the day, contrary to the nurse's wishes.

Period of Warm Attachment:
Then, when Paul was approximately one year old, his mother returned home from the hospital and replaced Paul's nurse as his caregiver. Fortunately for Paul, his mother—who identified with helpless creatures—became extremely attached to him and provided him with extra, if not excessive, care and attachment.

States Involving a Failure of Ego Integration:
Nevertheless, as would be predicted for a child who had been deprived of empathic care during infancy, Paul developed poorly. He displayed a failure to thrive so that by the age of fourteen years, he had reached a height of only four feet, two inches. Additionally, he remained awkward in his manual dexterity, was not able to throw a ball as other boys could, and started off at the bottom of his class in kindergarten and first grade.

Paul tried very hard to be a "good boy" in school, as is typical of those deprivational children who will do anything to get praise. In fact, he received the "blue ribbon" for being the most orderly child in the kindergarten class where he insisted on keeping a little table stacked with books "neat as a pin." However, Paul's reaction formation efforts to put order into his poorly integrated life failed to bring him mastery in his work. In the first grade he could not keep up with his class in reading. Furthermore, by the age of eight years, his restriction associated with his efforts to control his state of mental disorder and disorganization failed to the extent that he could not read, he could not spell, and failed in arithmetic.

Even though his reaction formation efforts were not earning him even passing grades in schoolwork, however, they did earn for him an A in conduct and an A in effort.

Then, as Paul turned nine, his reaction formation efforts to succeed began to bear fruit, and in the fifth grade he began to work compulsively, addictively, until he reached honor grades and became a top student in his class. Such reaction formation efforts were not without a price, however. He became entrenched in neurotically compulsive behavior. In order to do well he would do his homework hour after hour at home, sometimes until midnight, in an attempt to finish it perfectly. The conflict between (1) his underlying disintegrated, disorderly, messy tendencies of turning away from his work, and (2) his superimposed reaction formation behavior was revealed by the constant mistakes which intruded into his homework papers. These mistakes would drive him to do each sheet of homework over and over again until his final papers were correct, while the floor became literally covered with rejected papers. This compulsive behavior was repeated every night, together with an interminable ritual of lining his clothes in perfect order in an effort to assure himself that he was in control of his body as he was in control of his work.

The case of Paul illustrates psychoanalytic observations that reaction formations are characterized by rigidity and egocentricity—a rigidity and egocentricity which would be expected in the case of excessive restriction mobilized by attempts to counter states of chaos, disorganization, and impulsivity recorded under conditions of chronic early deprivation. According to Schafer, this rigidity based upon restriction of spontaneity is not "a mature, secure attitude of value. Because it blocks appropriate channels of discharge, this rigidity facilitates breakthroughs or infiltrations by the (underlying) rejected impulses" (Schafer, 1954, p. 347).

The case also illustrates the perfectionism of such reaction formation attempts to establish positive mastery control and power over the environment. The weaker the reaction formations and/or the stronger the triggered unintegrated, chaotic, fragmentary recordings established during early deprivation of empathic care, the more likely it would be that reaction formations may at least temporarily break down and fail as a supply line of pleasure. Supply line losses associated with reaction formation failures in turn reciprocally set the stage for the emergence of chaotic *HYPER States* which the reaction formation behavior had been covering. To combat incipient failure associated with the collapse of such reaction formations and the emergence of underlying states of disintegration, chaos, and disorder, a struggling child may seek ever-increasing perfectionism. "If I am perfect and if whatever I do is perfect, then I cannot fail in my goals of mastery and of control, or at least there will be less chance of my failing." In this way perfectionism may help maintain reaction formation goals of mastery as a (type B) compensatory supply line of pleasure.

The following case vignette further illustrates the rigid perfectionism which may accompany reaction formation attempts to establish mastery.

Case 29: Weil's Case of Francis (1989b, pp. 26–29)

Early Deprivation:
Francis experienced a particularly painful first three years of life during which his mother suffered prolonged depressions, withdrawal, and crying spells. She had no social contacts during these years and spent most of her time in bed. It was difficult for her to provide physical care for Francis, especially since, according to her own report, she was disoriented and confused during these years of his infancy. Often she would leave Francis helplessly screaming and cry-

ing for hours in his crib. Only after his third birthday was the mother able to provide him with more appropriate nurturance. During her own therapy the mother later revealed that she had been ridden with guilt with regard to the death of her own brother at the age of two-and-a-half years. Apparently recordings of her early overwhleming feelings were triggered during Francis's infancy (p. 26).

Compensatory Behavior Involving Turning Away from
Human Beings and Toward the Self:
At the age of thirteen, Francis found it very difficult to trust (and never did so during his three years of therapy). He often withdrew from his peers and preferred to quietly play alone or to spend time with the elders at church prayer meetings (p. 26).

Perfectionism:
Francis was obsessed with inner narcissistic feelings of devalued self-worth. He frequently expressed to his mother that he could not understand why she loved him at all, he was "no good," and so on. In order to compensate for these diffusely negative feelings, he rigidly and perfectionistically demanded A+ work from himself at school. Actually, Francis offered as his presenting problem his dissatisfaction with his school grades. Francis would take terrible fits during which he would keep hitting himself when he failed to get a perfect A+ mark. Shortly before his referral to the clinic, he became so furious that he hit the wall with his fists and tore his hair while calling himself dumb and saying he knew better than to act this way (p. 28).

Constructive Mastery as a Supply Line of Pleasure

Reaction formation appears equally to be a supply line and a defense. It is a defense insofar as it wards off painful feelings of chaos, disintegration, and disorganization. It is a supply line insofar as it forms the core for social behavior and mastery as a primary supply line of pleasure in the case of individuals who had been deprived of empathic care during infancy. Schafer reflects on this view when he writes,

> Reaction formations commonly take pseudo-sublimated, socially highly valued forms such as generosity, tenderness, sincerity, orderliness, conscientiousness, meticulousness, . . . bravery and altruism. The social rewards won by these reaction formations inevitably increase the tenacity with which people cling to them. That is to say, *more than a defensive function is served by reaction formation.* Generosity, tenderness, etc., are valuable means of interpersonal relationship and social gratification [Schafer, 1954, p. 347; emphasis added].

Pleasure from Mastery

Mastery may become an important source of pleasure as follows: goal mastery, great and small, according to common observation, releases pleasure when the goals are matched by perceptual fulfillment and when the goals are matched by expectations of fulfillment. The pleasure acquired from goal mastery, per se, is illustrated by the pleasure millions of people receive from sports. For example, pleasure is associated with perceptual goal fulfillment and anticipatory goal fulfillment associated with hitting a golf ball into a small hole. So is pleasure associated with the perceptual as well as anticipatory goal fulfillment of composing a piece of music, painting a picture, writing a piece of literature. In all these cases, not only goal fulfillment but also emotional expression becomes a source of pleasure. When goal fulfillment involves the acquisition of money and material goods, the chances of mastery becoming a supply line of pleasure become greatly enhanced for most individuals.

Once work, mastery, control, and power become an important source of pleasure, it becomes available as an addictive pleasure button for desperate individuals who are suffering from triggered recordings of deprivation, accompanied by chronic losses of pleasure, and feelings of emptiness. In such cases, the pleasure button associated with work can be relentlessly pressed as a means of restoring pleasure among individuals with such deprivational problems. Workaholic rigid reaction formation behavior in behalf of mastery and control among such individuals serves not only as a compensatory supply line of pleasure, but also a means for countering triggered recordings of underlying *HYPER States* of disorganization and of unintegrated, fragmented *HYPER* behavior (see Figure 10). Triggered recordings of deprivation, emptiness, and deficient pleasure can continually be countered when the pleasure button of mastery and creativeness is pressed without surcease (i.e., addictively). Additionally, the individual can derive compensatory pleasure from mastery much as he or she would derive compensatory pleasure from opiates. By means of the mastery pleasure button, the early deprived individual can claim: "I don't need empathy and love from any caregiver, present or past, for I can supply myself with any pleasure I may want. With mastery, and control, and power, and material wealth I can enjoy every comfort imaginable. Anything I need, from food, attention, sexual gratification, living in the 'lap of luxury,' I can purchase whenever and wherever I want. With mastery and power and money, people will come to my beck and call. I will enjoy control and power to dominate my environment for my own pleasures." Unfortunately, however, such reaction formation achievements of mastery often fail to cover up underlying triggered feelings of deprivation and emptiness, and all too often the workaholic may only ineffectively succeed in vanquishing his or her feelings of emptiness.

PREDICTION 5: ADOLESCENTS WHO HAD BEEN DEPRIVED OF EMPATHIC CARE DURING INFANCY AND WHO HAD LATER BEEN "RESCUED" BY EMPATHIC CAREGIVERS MAY SEEK TO RESCUE OTHER REJECTED HUMAN BEINGS (OR ANIMALS) AND THEREBY TRIGGER PLEASURABLE RECORDINGS OF BEING RESCUED THEMSELVES

Adolescents who had been moderately or minimally deprived of empathic care during infancy and who had later been rescued by an empathic caregiver, can be helped therapeutically by being encouraged to "identify with the rescuing person." Rescuing others provides a basis for triggering the adolescent's feelings of security associated with their own rescue early in their lives. When such individuals are hypersensitive, they may not be able to tolerate perceptions of other human beings exposed to rejection, deprivation, emptiness, and helplessness occurring in the world because such perceptions can trigger their own early recordings of traumatic deprivation and states of helplessness and distress. Intolerance for perceptions of rejection thereby may activate such individuals to fight suffering in the world around them. Thus, altruistic families or idealistic persons who have figured prominently within a child's or adolescent's life, for example, a political or religious idealist or an idealistic psychotherapist, slowly and gradually may help the child or adolescent to use altruism as a means of compensating for a history of moderate or minimal deprivation during infancy. Children and adolescents with a history of early deprivation may be helped to identify with the rescuer and to become outstanding individuals, altruistically and idealistically dedicated to helping the helpless, the weak, the poor, and the oppressed. This will form a basis for eliciting expectations of love and care in the world to counter their feelings of deprivation and a basis for creating a surrounding world in which the maternal instincts of empathic care can prevail.

According to this prediction, the disadvantages incurred by an individual's early deprivation of empathic care, under optimal conditions, may be converted to a socially beneficial intolerance for injustice meted upon the rejected members of society—a sublimated form of dealing with triggered feelings of deprivation.

However, for altruistic goals, hopes, and expectations to become a constructive supply line of pleasure, it is necessary for the goals to be based upon reality. Altruistic behavior which disregards reality can become a prominent constituent of psychotic behavior. Thus, altruistic ideals based upon delusionary fantasies and delusionary great expectations as supply lines of pleasure can provide a familiar core of psychotic thinking. It is not unusual to find a psychotic patient rambling on with altruistic delusions of glory in which he or she professes to be the altruistic savior of the world. Sometimes such a patient may be found expostulating his or her convictions in parks or on street corners. One can understand how an individual's fantasies of becoming the Messiah can provide great expectations of power, mastery, and control as well as expectations of a new world in which love and adulation will prevail. Such highly pleasurable fantasies then can easily fill a void of pleasure to become a primary supply line of pleasure. Sometimes there may exist a thin line between unrealistic great expectations of altruistic endeavor and realistic accomplishment. A patient struggling with a compensatory need to attain altruistic supply lines would therefore often require help in reaching and maintaining such goals via difficult and laborious pathways of reality accomplishment.

Social versus Asocial Supply Lines of Pleasure
Compensating for Early Deprivation of Empathic Care

Family, peer group, and societal customs and mores help determine what type of compensatory supply lines will predominate for a given individual with a history of early deprivation of empathic care. These customs will influence whether compensatory supply lines will be involved with (1) turning to pathological asocial behavior based on immediate gratification (e.g., as in the case of alcoholism); or, conversely, (2) constructive socially oriented behavior based upon a capacity for delayed gratification (e.g., as in the case of workaholic adjustments). In this connection, numerous researchers, for example, Rutter, Garmezy, and Anthony individually have observed that some children display severely pathological reactions to early deprivation, while other children appear to be "resilient" and to adapt more successfully (Rutter, 1979, pp. 295, 297; Anthony, 1983, pp. 105–106; Garmezy, Masten, and Tellegen, 1984, p. 109; Rutter, 1987, pp. 316, 325).

The following conditions pertaining to the presence or absence of deprivation of empathic care during the first year of life, interacting with conditions pertaining to the presence or absence of deprivation during and after the second year of life, help to determine what forms of supply lines are established.

1. The greater the empathic care during the first year of life, the greater the chance there will be maintained and reinforced some empathically resonant socialized compensatory supply lines.

1a. The less the empathic care during the first year of life, the greater the chance that the compensatory supply lines will involve asocial turning away from other human beings.

2. The greater the emphasis upon empathy and social controls during the second year of life and thereafter, the greater the chance for establishing reaction formations and sublimations to counter asocial effects of early deprivation.

2a. The less the emphasis upon empathy and social controls during the second year of life and thereafter, the less the chance for establishing sufficient reaction formations and sublimations to counter the asocial effects of early deprivation.

These hypotheses suggest that the effectiveness of reaction formations and sublimations as a source for establishing socialized controls depends upon ego development as a function of empathic care during the first and second year of life. When underlying primitive instinctual supply lines are strong and/or superimposed reaction formations and sublimations are weak, underlying impulsive asocial behavior would be expected to break through (Kernberg, 1975, p. 29). Thus, an unstable balance frequently may be set up between the subject's dependence upon asocial vs. socialized compensatory supply lines—an alternation or a coexistence of the socialized and asocial forms of compensation. For example, reference has already been made to Paul, a little boy in Anna Freud's Hampstead group of children deprived during infancy. Paul would alternate between highly socialized and withdrawn asocial compensatory forms of adjustment. Anna Freud writes:

> Paul, in his good periods, was an excellent member of the group, friendly, attentive, and helpful toward children and adults. . . . But when he went through one of his phases of compulsive sucking and masturbating, the whole environment including the other children, lost their significance for

him. He ceased to care about them, just as he ceased to eat or play by himself [A. Freud and Dann, 1951, p. 148].

Similarly, Kernberg presents the case of a patient who alternated between (1) states of emotional upheaval involving anger and depression, chaotic relations with men, as well as alcoholism and drug addiction, and (2) an "empty," "friendly" but detached behavior (Kernberg, 1975, pp. 94, 95). Kernberg refers to such dependence upon incompatible supply lines, one social and the other asocial, in terms of a split ego effect. He writes, "With these patients it is not a matter of searching for unconscious repressed material but [rather] bridging and integrating what appears on the surface to be two or more emotionally independent but alternately active ego states" (Kernberg, 1975, p. 96).

Numerous famous individuals who show the earmarks of early deprivation display a coexistence or alternation of (1) creative, constructive socialized and (2) disruptive, self-centered, asocial compensatory supply lines of pleasure. For example, Marcel Proust, like a frozen neglected baby, neurotically longed for his mother's care, and wore his overcoat at social gatherings to keep himself warm (Lampl-de Groot, 1976, p. 280). When his mother didn't kiss him on an occasion when he was seven years old, he became wildly distraught (Straus, 1980, p. 7). Additionally, Proust displayed withdrawal (p. 2) and "agonies of introspection" (p. 49), as well as a turning compulsively to his body via hypochondria even when he looked quite well (pp. 2, 5, 6, 86)—all examples of exaggerated turning away from others and toward himself and his body as supply lines of pleasure (see chapter 7, Figure 10). Eventually he dealt with his feelings of neglect by writing outstanding novels, but concomitantly became driven by "degrading" addictive homosexual promiscuity (Lampl-de Groot, 1976, p. 280). Straus suggested that writing enabled

Proust "to reduce a disorderly succession of images ... to coherence, proportion and order" (1980, p. 48). Straus adds that such a "split" personality in general has been alleged to be a characteristic of hypersensitive, creative people (p. 92). Sinclair Lewis provides another example of a famous figure who sought to compensate for his recorded feelings of rejection, deprivation, and aloneness by means of great ego achievements in writing outstanding novels about middle-class America in the 1930s. However, even after he received the Nobel Prize for literature, he remained riddled with feelings of deprivation and rejection and thereupon turned impulsively to alcoholism as an asocial, self-destructive compensatory supply line of pleasure (Schorer, 1961, pp. 3, 539, 594, 607, 629, 674, 806).

SUMMATION AND RECOMMENDATIONS
FOR RESEARCH

Thus, clinical findings draw attention to a myriad of symptoms associated with chronic deprivation of empathic care during infancy, symptoms based upon exaggerated *deficiencies of pleasure* and exaggerated *HYPER* and/or *HYPO States*. Among these are exaggerated feelings of emptiness; exaggerated seeking of love; exaggerated egocentric preoccupations with controlling and manipulating the environment; exaggerated sensual and/or hypochondriacal preoccupations with the individual's own body and body products; exaggerated sexuality; exaggerated withdrawal into states of sleep or lethargy. Such symptoms, at their worst, may reach psychotic proportions, for example, when depletion of pleasure is accompanied by *HYPER States* of chaotic disintegration or *HYPO States* of debilitation disrupting work, learning, and social functioning. Such states become especially pathological during adolescence when there occurs the instinctual reactivation and amplification of deprivational symptoms recorded during infancy. Symptoms at their best may lead to "magnificent obsessions" involving workaholic behavior as well as creative and/or altruistic contributions to civilization. In between these extremes appear the pathological addictive disturbances and borderline states and split ego states in which socially oriented behavior alternates with asocially oriented behavior, and behavior that is constructive alternates with behavior that is self-destructive or destructive to others.

Any of these predictions are available for long-term clinical investigation. For example, the clinical findings presented in this chapter lead to a recommendation that a long-term study be established over a period of twenty years to investigate the relation between chronic deprivation of empathic care during infancy and the emergence of addictive symptoms during adolescence and early adulthood. Definitions of both independent and dependent variables in terms of operational measurements throughout this monograph would facilitate a scientific approach for such an investigation.

The advantages of a twenty-year investigation of early deprivation of empathic care as an antecedent for the addictions are unmistakable, for there is not yet available an accepted environmental theory to help explain the etiology of alcoholism, involuntary homosexuality, compulsive neuroses, or unfeeling delinquency. Today, a preponderance of attention has been focused upon the constitutional backgrounds of these disturbances. Therefore, we are faced with a definite diagnostic need for controlled investigations to delineate more clearly some of the environmental sources of these most baffling emotional disorders.

However, the greatest advantage of a long-term investigation of the predicted symptoms arising from deprivation of empathic care among infants would involve its contribution to the prevention of these symptoms. For example, if alcoholism, drug addiction, involuntary homosexuality, schizoid withdrawal, and unfeeling delinquency all prove to be at least in part dependent upon a history of emotional deprivation during infancy, then a massive public health endeavor to bring better empathic attention into the lives of infants should prove effective in helping us reduce the prevalence of these pathological disorders affecting millions of human beings.

Some Relations Between Hospitalism and Anaclitic Depression

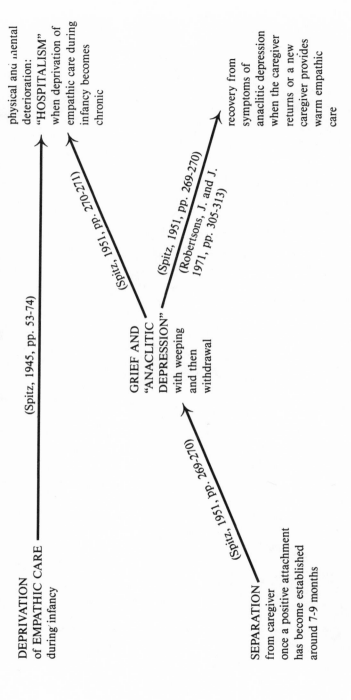

DEPRIVATION
of EMPATHIC CARE
during infancy

(Spitz, 1945, pp. 53-74)

physical and mental
deterioration:
"HOSPITALISM"
when deprivation of
empathic care during
infancy becomes
chronic

(Spitz, 1951, pp. 270-271)

GRIEF AND
"ANACLITIC
DEPRESSION"
with weeping
and then
withdrawal

(Spitz, 1951, pp. 269-270)

(Robertsons, J. and J.
1971, pp. 305-313)

recovery from
symptoms of
anaclitic depression
when the caregiver
returns or a new
caregiver provides
warm empathic
care

SEPARATION
from caregiver
once a positive attachment
has become established
around 7-9 months

(Spitz, 1951, pp. 269-270)

APPENDIX 2

The Supply Lines of Pleasure and the Definition of the Infant's Self-Concept

During the first two years of life, there gradually occurs an opportunity for the growing infant to encounter a series of positive and negative "primary experiences" pertaining to supplies of pleasure, care, and protection. Recordings of such primary experiences pertaining to care of the infant occurring during the infant's first two years of life then would provide a basis for the infant's supply line self-images or self-representations:

1. The infant's body as a source for visceral, tactile, and kinesthetic visual pleasurable or unpleasurable states would provide a foundation for recordings of the infant's body image (Jacobson, 1953, p. 56; Fenichel, 1954, p. 29).
2. The parental ego as a source of pleasurable or unpleasurable states would provide for recordings of the infant's being cared for by the parent's ego, that is, recordings of "being pleasurably (or unpleasurably) cared for" or of "being (or not being) loved." (For additional comments on this subject, see Nachman and Stern, 1984, pp. 95–96).

3. In accordance with White's conclusions, the infant's own rudimentary ego as a source of pleasurable or unpleasurable states would provide for recordings of the infant's own efforts, that is, recordings involving manipulation, control, mastery, power, competence, success, effectance, efficacy, a basis for a self-concept of adequacy or inadequacy (White, 1963, pp. 37–39). In connection with such processes, Emde summarizes the literature pertaining to self-awareness, self-recognition, wilfulness, and autonomy (Emde, 1984, p. 39).

At first, the infant must be primarily aware of its own bodily feelings and sensations (visceral and kinesthetic), in association with its visual and tactile contacts with its mother (as it suckles at the mother's breast, is kept warm, is cuddled, rocked, bathed, kissed, and diapered). In this regard, Phyllis Greenacre has observed that the infant's contacts with its own body and with the mother's breast often occur simultaneously: "The baby, simultaneously with sucking at the breast or bottle may play with its hands over the mother's breasts or clothing, and may later develop a rhythmic touching of its own cheek or pulling at the lobe of its own ear, or touching a lock of its hair, or the edge of the blanket" (Greenacre, 1959, p. 70). It is, therefore, likely that for the first six months of life the infant's instinctual recordings of pleasure in association with the parental ego, its own body, and its own rudimentary ego must be intimately fused. Only gradually, as the infant grows, would there occur an opportunity for the formation of highly differentiated cerebral, cognitive representations of these sources of supply and protection (White, 1963, pp. 50–51).

Such primary and permanent emotional recordings involving body image, being loved, ego mastery, control, competence, or motor power as supply lines of pleasure provivde a basis for expectations which can be triggered later in life. These formulations account for the hypotheses that:

1. Children who have been cared for securely and empathically as infants will grow up with basic convictions that they are in a caring world and with inner optimistic expectations that they will be loved.
2. Children who as infants have been helped to succeed in their efforts to gain abundant supplies of pleasure, will be likely to grow up with expectations that their own endeavors will bring pleasure and reward, that is, with basic optimistic convictions that they have the capacity to succeed.

Such positive expectations and convictions would then be able to be triggered later in the child's or adult's life by even minor events which in some small way are equivalent to the initial experiences recorded.

Conversely,

1. Children who have been deprived, rejected, and treated punitively during infancy would be likely to grow up with expectations of rejection and a basic (paranoidlike) conviction that they are surrounded by, enmeshed in, an uncaring hostile environment (Steele, 1980, p. 57).
2. Children who have been placed in the position of helpless ego failure during infancy will grow up with pessimistic expectations that their actions will eventuate in failure.

Such negative expectations and convictions would then be able to be triggered later in the child's or adult's life by even minor events which in some way are equivalent to the initial experiences recorded.

The Supply Lines of Pleasure and Self-Esteem

Recordings of reactions taking place during infancy provide a basis not only for the formation of the individual's self-representations and self-expectations (i.e., self-concept), but also for the establishment of its inner feelings of self-esteem. *Self-esteem* is a term which implies the degree to which rewarding feelings of pleasure versus unrewarding feelings of unpleasure are associated with an individual's self-image, self-representation, or self-expectations; that is, the degree to which the individual's body image, image of being cared for, and/or image of mastery are associated with pleasure or unpleasure.

This formulation that self-esteem varies as a function of these recorded sources of supply of pleasure is in keeping with observations reported within the psychoanalytic literature. Table IV lists some pertinent references. Table V lists a number of interchangeable terms which have been used to refer to self-esteem in terms of pleasurable and/or unpleasurable feelings attached to the self image.

Furthermore, in accordance with the hypotheses presented in this text, a pleasurable or unpleasurable self-concept, or a positive or negative self-esteem, would derive from two sources: (1) pleasure or displeasure from the subject's current supply lines, and (2) pleasure or displeasure recorded during infancy and triggered by somewhat similar conditions in the present environment. According to this formulation, an individual's states of self-pleasure or self-

TABLE IV

Self-Esteem as a Function of
Types A, B, and C Supply Lines of Pleasure
(References within the Psychoanalytic Literature)

1. positive self-esteem
a function of the body
as a supply line of
pleasure

Fenichel, O. (1945, p. 72)

Freud, S. (1913, p. 336)

2. positive self-esteem
a function of being
loved as a supply
line of pleasure

White, R. (1963, p. 127)

Fenichel, O. (1945, p. 41)

Sroufe, L. (1989, p. 76)

3. positive self-esteem[1]
a function of mastery,
power, control, efficacy, effectiveness,
accomplishment as a
supply line of pleasure[2]

Fenichel, O. (1954, p. 94)

White, R. (1963, p. 125)

Mittelmann, B. (1954, p. 156)

Mittelmann, B. (1957, pp. 300, 310)

[1] Which may be referred to as self-regard.
[2] Fenichel referred to "narcissistic supplies" in relation to self-esteem. It is this phrase which suggested the concept of "supply lines of pleasure" upon which this manuscript is based (Fenichel, 1945, pp. 41, 136, 137).

TABLE V

Terms Referring to Recordings of the Self
Associated with Pleasure and Displeasure

The degree to which the primary supply lines of the self are associated with pleasure (*pleasurable* feelings about *self*):	The degree to which the primary supply lines of the self are associated with displeasure (*unpleasurable* feelings about *self*):
elevated self-esteem	reduced self-esteem
positive self-esteem	negative self-esteem
elevated self-regard	depressed self-regard
feeling "good" about the self	feeling "bad" about the self
liking one's self	disliking one's self
feeling proud of one's self	feeling ashamed of one's self

esteem may appear to be incompatible with current reality when a slight loss of a current supply line may trigger extreme losses of pleasure associated with feelings of deprivation and emptiness recorded during infancy.

Such connections have already been observed by Steele who concluded that early deprivation of empathic care is conducive to general "lack of pleasure" (Steele, 1986, p. 287), "low self-esteem," "impaired self concept" (1986, pp. 286, 289), and associated depression (p. 287).

The Arousal and Pleasure Axes and the Infant's States of Depression and Agitation

Depression and agitation are definable in terms of the two axes of emotion that can be measured from the time of early infancy onward: (1) the arousal and (2) the pleasure–displeasure–distress axes. Depression can be defined as a persistent *HYPO State* of arousal accompanied by a persistent *loss of pleasure* (American Psychiatric Association, 1980, pp. 213–214).

Thus, the DSM-III definition of depression focuses upon (1) *HYPO States* involving "loss of energy," "fatigue," "slowed thinking," "hypersomnia," and/or "poor appetite" (i.e., anorexia), combined with (2) "loss of pleasure," a "dysphoric mood in all or almost all usual activities and pastimes. A dysphoric mood is characterized by . . . [feelings of being] sad, blue, hopeless, low, down in the dumps" (American Psychiatric Association, 1980, pp. 213–214).[1]

---

[1]The DSM-III definition of generalized anxiety parallels the definition presented in this appendix more exactly than does the definition presented in DSM-III-R (1987).

On the other hand, the DSM-III definition of agitation focuses upon a persistent *HYPER State* accompanied by a loss of pleasure and by a reciprocal elevation of displeasure or distress. In line with this definition, the DSM-III definition of generalized anxiety (the equivalent of generalized agitation) focuses upon

> *HYPER States* involving
> "*motor tension*: shakiness, jitteriness, jumpiness, trembling, tension, muscle aches, . . . inability to relax, . . . fidgeting, restlessness, easy startle"; "vigilance: hyperattentiveness resulting in distractability, difficulty in concentrating, insomnia, feeling 'on edge,' irritability, impatience" (American Psychiatric Association, 1980, p. 233); and
> "*autonomic hyperactivity*: . . . heart pounding or racing, high resting pulse, [high] respiratory rate," "diarrhea" (p. 233); together with
> "*apprehensive expectations*: [expected loss of pleasure with reciprocal] anticipation of misfortune to self and others" (p. 233).

These descriptions of depression and agitation are in keeping with the findings of Beck (1970, pp. 16, 40) and of Beck and Emery (1985, pp. 14, 26).

The Supply Lines of Pleasure and the Concepts of Agitation and Anxiety

Freud's basic formulations pertaining to "ego-anxiety" presented in "Inhibitions, Symptoms, and Anxiety" (1926) offer a definition of anxiety which pertains to emotional loss: loss of uterine care; loss of a mother's care; loss of genital sources of pleasure; as well as loss pertaining to other body parts and products as a source of pleasure. Freud notes that the term *anxiety* implies expectations of danger (1926, p. 166) and more specifically indicated that such expectations pertain to:

> loss of a mother or a mother's love (pp. 143, 170),
> helplessness (i.e., loss of ego mastery) (p. 166),
> castration-loss of the penis and of other pleasure-giving
> body parts and products (pp. 129–130).

In this connection, Freud went on to suggest that anxiety also appears at birth entailing loss of uterine sources of bliss (1926, pp. 130, 138).

In brief, Freud's term *anxiety* primarily refers to loss of key sources of pleasure.[1]

What a trigger theory of emotion adds is an emphasis upon the part played by early deprivation of empathic care synergistically interacting with the effects of current losses of supply lines of pleasure as instrumental in the etiology of generalized overwhelming states of agitation or anxiety. Such an approach would account for Freud's observation that some individuals react to a loss with a "signal anxiety"; that is, a minimal emotional disturbance which warns the subject to take helpful steps to compensate for such a loss; whereas other individuals react to a loss with the triggering of overwhelming anxiety which disrupts cognitive (ego) attempts to deal with these losses calmly and constructively. According to the trigger theory of emotional activation presented in chapter 6, reactions of extreme deprivation and overwhelming *HYPER States* of agitation recorded during infancy would subsequently be triggered in the form of overwhelming agitation or free-floating anxiety (*HYPER States*), whereas reactions of minimal deprivation associated with comforting by a caring parent during infancy would subsequently be triggered in the form of minimal amounts of agitation which Freud referred to as signal anxiety. For additional observations pertaining to this subject, see Yorke and Wiseberg (1976, pp. 130–131).

---

[1] The term *anxiety* which pertains to loss of sources of pleasure contrasts with the term *fear* which pertains to expectation of physical pain or discomfort; for example, usually people speak of fears (not anxieties) of being beaten, fears of being bitten or stung, fears of being burned—all sources of physical pain—but anxieties pertain to expectation of loss of supply lines of pleasure.

Some Contrasts and Similarities Between Compensatory Supply Lines and Defenses

The equivalence of (diffuse) "anxiety" as defined by Freud and "agitation" as defined in appendix 5 suggests the following relation of defenses and compensatory supply lines of pleasure:

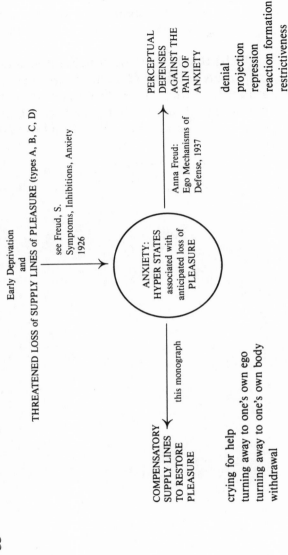

Early Deprivation
and
THREATENED LOSS of SUPPLY LINES of PLEASURE (types A, B, C, D)

see Freud, S.
Symptoms, Inhibitions, Anxiety
1926

ANXIETY:
HYPER STATES
associated with
anticipated loss of
PLEASURE

Anna Freud:
Ego Mechanisms of
Defense, 1937

PERCEPTUAL
DEFENSES
AGAINST THE
PAIN OF
ANXIETY

denial
projection
repression
reaction formation
restrictiveness

COMPENSATORY
SUPPLY LINES   this monograph
TO RESTORE
PLEASURE

crying for help
turning away to one's own ego
turning away to one's own body
withdrawal

The Relation of Early Deprivation of Empathic Care, Compensatory Supply Lines of Pleasure, and Narcissism

Type D compensatory supply lines of pleasure involving the deprived infant's exaggerated turning away emotionally from other human beings and toward its self via excessive withdrawal into uterinelike states of lethargy and sleep provide a basis for disturbances that are referred to as "uterine narcissism" or "primary narcissism" (Freud, 1921, p. 130; Greenacre, 1945, pp. 46–47).

Type C compensatory supply lines of pleasure involving the deprived infant's exaggerated turning away emotionally from other human beings and toward its self via excessive contact with its erogenous and erotic body parts and body products provide a basis for disturbances that are referred to as "body narcissism" (Freud, 1905, p. 218 fn 3; Ellis, 1928).

Type B compensatory supply lines of pleasure involving the deprived infant's exaggerated turning away emotionally from other human beings and toward its self via excessive dependency upon its own ego provide a basis for disturbances which might be appropriately referred to as "egocentric narcissism," a form of secondary narcissism (Freud, 1914, p. 75).

Type A compensatory supply lines of pleasure involving the deprived infant's exaggerated screaming demands for care from its caregiver, demands for its self, provide a basis for disturbances which might be appropriately referred to as "anaclitic narcissism," "hyper leaning-on type of narcissism" (Freud, 1914, p. 87, fn 2). See Fenichel regarding narcissistic supply lines (1945, p. 137).

Thus, an investigation of the deprived infant's turning away from others and turning primarily to its self should be able to shed light upon the etiology of the narcissistic disorders.

References

Adler, A. (1956), *The Individual Psychology of Alfred Adler*, ed. H. Ansbacher & R. Ansbacher. New York: Basic Books.

Adler, G. (1985), *Borderline Psychopathology and Its Treatment*. New York: Jason Aronson.

Ainsworth, M. (1966), The effects of maternal deprivation, a review. In: *Deprivation of Maternal Care, a Reassessment of Its Effects*, ed. M. Ainsworth, R. G. Andry, R. G. Harlow, S. Lebovici, M. Mead, D. G. Prugh, & B. Wootton. In conjunction with John Bowlby's *Maternal Care and Mental Health*. New York: Schocken Books, pp. 289–357.

—— Bell, S., & Stayton, D. (1974), Infant–mother attachment and social development. In: *Integration of a Child into a Social World*, ed. M. Richards. London: Cambridge University Press, pp. 99–135.

—— Blehar, M., Waters, E., & Wall, S. (1978), *Patterns of Attachment*. Hillsdale, NJ: Lawrence Erlbaum.

Altman, J. (1967), Postnatal growth and differentiation of the mammalian brain. In: *The Neurosciences*, ed. G. C. Quarton, T. Melnechuk, & F. O. Schmitt. New York: Rockefeller University Press, pp. 723–743.

American Psychiatric Association (1980), *The Diagnostic and Statistical Manual of Mental Disorders*. Washington, DC: American Psychiatric Press.

—— (1987), *The Diagnostic and Statistical Manual of Mental Disorders* (DSM-III-R). Washington, DC: American Psychiatric Press.

Anisman, H., & Sklar, L. (1979), Catecholamine depletion in mice upon reexposure to stress. *J. Compar. & Physiol. Psychol.*, 93:610–625.

Anthony, E. J. (1983), Infants in a crazy environment: Psychotic parents. In: *Frontiers of Infant Psychiatry*, Vol. 1, ed. J. Call, E. Galenson, & R. Tyson. New York: Basic Books, pp. 95–107.

—— (1984), The influence babies bring to bear on their upbringing. In: *Frontiers of Infant Psychiatry*, Vol. 2, ed. J. Call, E. Galenson, & R. Tyson. New York: Basic Books, pp. 259–266.

191

Bakwin, H. (1949), Emotional deprivation in infants. *J. Pediat.*, 35:512–521.

Beck. A. (1970). *Depression, Causes and Treatment.* Philadelphia: University of Pennsylvania Press.

—— Emery, G. (1985), *Anxiety Disorders and Phobias.* New York: Basic Books.

Belluzzi, J. D., & Stein, L. (1977), Enkephalin may mediate euphoria and drive-reduction reward. *Nature,* 266:556–558.

Bender, L. (1935), Emotional problems in children. *Proceedings of the Second Institute on the Exceptional Child.* Langhorne, PA: The Child Research Clinic of the Woods Schools, 2:49–64.

—— (1975), A career of clinical research in child psychiatry. In: *Explorations in Child Psychiatry,* ed. E. J. Anthony. New York: Plenum Press, pp. 419–462.

Benedek, T. (1956), The psychobiological aspects of mothering. *Amer. J. Orthopsychiat.,* 26:272–278.

Benjamin, J. D. (1961), The innate and experiential in development. In: *Lectures on Experimental Psychiatry,* ed. H. W. Brosin. Pittsburgh: University of Pittsburgh Press, pp. 19–42.

Beres, D., & Obers, S. (1950), The effects of extreme deprivation in infancy on psychic structure in adolescence: A study in ego development. *The Psychoanalytic Study of the Child,* 5:212–235. New York: International Universities Press.

Bergman, P., & Escalona, S. (1949), Unusual sensitivities in very young children. *The Psychoanalytic Study of the Child,* 3/4:333–352. New York: International Universities Press.

Bishop, M., Elder, S. T., & Heath, R. (1964), Attempted control of operant behavior in man with intracranial self-stimulation. In: *The Role of Pleasure in Behavior,* ed. R. Heath, New York: Hoeber/Harper & Row, p. 70.

Blatt, S. J. (1974), Levels of object representation in anaclitic and introjective depression. *The Psychoanalytic Study of the Child,* 29:107–157. New Haven, CT: Yale University Press.

Blumstein, P., & Schwartz, P. (1983), *American Couples.* New York: Morrow.

Bond, E., & Partridge, G. E. (1926), Post-encephalic behavior disorders in boys and their management in a hospital. *Amer. J. Psychiat.,* 6:3–103.

Bonnet, K. A., Hiller, J. M., & Simon, E. J. (1976), The effects of chronic opiate treatment and social isolation on opiate receptors in the rodent brain. In: *Opiates and Endogenous Opioid Peptides,* ed. S. Archer, H. O. J. Collier, A. Goldstein, H. W. Kosterlitz, E. J. Simon, H. Takagi, & L. Terenius. New York: Elsevier/North Holland, 1976, pp. 335–343.

Bowlby, J. (1951), *Maternal Care and Mental Health.* World Health Organization, Vol. 3. New York: Schocken, 1966.

—— (1969), Attachment, Vol. 1. In: *Attachment and Loss.* New York: Basic Books.

—— (1973), Separation, Vol. 2. In: *Attachment and Loss*. New York: Basic Books.

—— (1980), Loss: Sadness and depression, Vol. 3. In: *Attachment and Loss*. London: Hogarth Press; New York: Basic Books; Harmondsworth, UK: Penguin, 1981.

—— (1988), *A Secure Base*. New York: Basic Books.

Bradley, C. (1937), The behavior of children receiving benzedrine. *Amer. J. Psychiat.*, 94:577–585.

Brazelton, T. B. (1969), *Infants and Mothers: Differences in Development*. New York: Delta/Seymour Lawrence & Delacorte/Seymour Lawrence.

—— (1980), Behavioral competence of the newborn infant. In: *Parent–Infant Relationships*, ed. P. Taylor. New York: Grune & Stratton, pp. 69–85.

—— (1983), Precursors for the development of emotions in early infancy. In: *Emotion, Theory, Research and Experience*, Vol. 2, ed. R. Plutchik & H. Kellerman. New York: Academic Press, pp. 35–55.

—— Als, H. (1979), Four early stages in the development of mother–infant interaction. *The Psychoanalytic Study of the Child*, 34:349–369. New Haven, CT: Yale University Press.

—— Koslowski, B., & Main, M. (1974), The origins of reciprocity (the early mother–infant interaction). In: *The Effect of the Infant on Its Caregiver*, ed. M. Lewis & L. Rosenblum. New York: John Wiley, pp. 49–76.

Brody, J. (1983), Emotional deprivation seen as devastating form of child abuse. *New York Times*, December 20:C1.

Brody, S., & Axelrad, S. (1970), *Anxiety and Ego Formation in Infancy*. New York: International Universities Press.

—— —— (1978), *Mothers, Fathers, Children*. New York: International Universities Press.

Brutkowski, S. (1964), Prefrontal cortex and drive inhibition. In: *The Frontal Granular Cortex and Behavior*, ed. J. M. Warren & K. Akert. New York: McGraw-Hill, pp. 242–270.

Buxbaum, E. (1960), Hair pulling and fetishism. *The Psychoanalytic Study of the Child*, 15:243–260. New York: International Universities Press.

Cannon, W. B. (1939), *The Wisdom of the Body*. New York: W. W. Norton.

Cantwell, D. (1972), Psychiatric illness in the families of hyperactive children. *Arch. Gen. Psychiat.*, 27:414–417.

—— (1975), Genetic studies of hyperactive children. In: *Genetic Research in Psychiatry*, ed. R. Fieve, D. Rosenthal, & H. Brill. Baltimore: Johns Hopkins University Press, pp. 273–280.

Carnes, P. (1983), *Out of the Shadows, Understanding Sexual Addiction*. Minneapolis: CompCare Publications.

Chapin, H. D. (1915), A plea for accurate statistics in infants' institutions. *Arch. Pediat.*, 32:724–726.

Clarke, A. D. B., & Clarke, A. M. (1960), Some recent advances in the study of early deprivation. *J. Child Psychol. & Psychiat.*, 1:26–36.

Clements, S., & Peters, J. (1962), Minimal brain dysfunctions in the school-age child. *Arch. Gen. Psychiat.*, 6:185–197.

Cohen, D. J., Shaywitz, S. E., Young, J. G., & Shaywitz, B. (1982), Borderline syndromes and attention deficit disorders of childhood. In: *The Borderline Child*, ed. K. Robson. New York: McGraw-Hill, pp. 198–221.

Coleman, R. V., & Provence, S. (1957), Environmental retardation (hospitalism) in infants living in families. *Pediatrics*, 19:285–292.

Cross, B. A., & Harris, G. W. (1952), The role of the neurohypophysis in the milk-ejection reflex. *J. Endocrinol.*, 8:148–161.

Delgado, J. M. R. (1967), Limbic system and free behavior. In: *Progress in Brain Research*, Vol. 27, ed. W. R. Adey & T. Tokizane. Amsterdam: Elsevier, pp. 48–68.

Dember, W. N., & Earl, R. M. (1957), Analysis of exploratory, manipulatory and curiosity behaviors. *Psychol. Rev.*, 64:91–96.

Demos, V. (1984), Empathy and affect: Reflections on infant experience. In: *Empathy*, Vol. 2, ed. J. Lichtenberg, M. Bornstein, & D. Silver. Hillsdale, NJ: Analytic Press, pp. 9–34.

DeVore, I. (1963), Mother–infant relations in free-ranging baboons. In: *Maternal Behavior in Mammals*, ed. H. Rheingold. New York: John Wiley, pp. 305–335.

Diamond, S., Balvin, R., & Diamond, F. (1963), *Inhibition and Choice*. New York: Harper & Row.

du Pan, R. M., & Roth, S. (1955), The psychologic development of a group of children brought up in a hospital type residential nursery. *J. Pediat.*, 47:124–129.

Durfee, H., & Wolf, K. (1934), Anstaltspflege und Entwicklung im 1. Lebensjahr. *Zeitschr. für Kinderforschung*, 42:273–320.

Easser, R. (1974), Empathic inhibition and psychoanalytic technique. *Psychoanal. Quart.*, 43:557–580.

Ebaugh, F. G. (1923), Neuropsychiatric sequelae of acute epidemic encephalitis in children. *Amer. J. Dis. Child.*, 25:89–97.

Eckstein-Schlossmann, E. (1926), Zur Frage des Hospitalismus in Säuglingsanstalten. *Zeitschr. für Kinderheilkunde*, 42:31–38.

Egeland, B. (1985), The consequences of physical and emotional neglect on the development of young children. Paper presented at the Neglect Symposium, Washington, DC, November 9, 1985, pp. 1–19.

—— Erickson, M. (1987), Psychologically unavailable caregiving. In: *Psychological Maltreatment of Children and Youth*, ed. M. R. Brassard, R. Germain, & S. N. Hart. New York: Pergamon Press, pp. 110–120.

Ellis, H. (1928), *Studies on the Psychology of Sex*, Vol. 7. Philadelphia.

Emde, R. (1980a), Emotional availability: A reciprocal reward system for infants and parents with implications for prevention of psychosocial disorders. In: *Parent–Infant Relationships*, ed. P. Taylor. New York: Grune & Stratton, pp. 87–115.

—— (1980b), Levels of meaning for infant emotions. In: *Development of Cognition, Affect and Social Relations*, The Minnesota Symposia on

Child Psychology, Vol. 13, ed. W. A. Collins. Hillsdale, NJ: Lawrence Erlbaum, pp. 1–37.
—— (1983), The prerepresentational self and its affective core. *The Psychoanalytic Study of the Child,* 38:165–192. New Haven, CT: Yale University Press.
—— (1984), The affective self: Continuities and transformations from infancy. In: *Frontiers of Infant Psychiatry,* Vol. 2, ed. J. Call, E. Galenson, & R. Tyson. New York: Basic Books, pp. 38–54.
—— Gaensbauer, T., & Harmon, R. (1976), Emotional Expression in Infancy: A Biobehavioral Study. *Psychological Issues,* Vol. 10, No. 1, Monogr. 37. New York: International Universities Press.
—— Harmon, R., & Good, W. (1986), Depressive feelings in children: A transactional model for research. In: *Depression in Young People,* ed. M. Rutter, C. Izard, & P. Read. New York: Guilford Press, pp. 135–160.
—— Kligman, D., Reich, J., & Wade, T. (1978), Emotional expression in infancy: Initial studies of social signaling and an emergent model. In: *The Development of Affect,* ed. M. Lewis & L. Rosenblum. New York: Plenum Press, pp. 125–148.
Engle, G. (1962), Anxiety and depression-withdrawal: The primary affects of unpleasure. *Internat. J. Psycho-Anal.,* 43:89–97.
Erickson, M., & Egeland, B. (1987), A developmental view of the psychological consequences of maltreatment. *School Psychol. Rev.,* 16:2, pp. 156–168.
Erikson, E. (1968), *Identity, Youth and Crisis.* New York: W. W. Norton.
Escalona, S. (1954), Problems of infantile neurosis. *The Psychoanalytic Study of the Child,* 9:45–46. New York: International Universities Press.
—— (1963), Patterns of infantile experience and the developmental process. *The Psychoanalytic Study of the Child,* 18:197–244. New York: International Universities Press.
Fairbairn, W. (1940), Schizoid factors in personality. In: *Object-Relations Theory of the Personality.* London: Tavistock, 1952, pp. 3–27.
Fenichel, O. (1945), *Psychoanalytic Theory of the Neurosis.* New York: W. W. Norton.
—— (1954), Early stages of ego development. In: *The Collected Papers of Otto Fenichel,* Vol. 2. New York: W. W. Norton, pp. 25–48.
Ferholt, J., & Provence, S. (1976), Diagnosis and treatment of an infant with psychophysiological vomiting. *The Psychoanalytic Study of the Child,* 31:439–459. New Haven, CT: Yale University Press.
Flint, B. M. (1966), *The Child and the Institution: A Study of Deprivation and Recovery.* Toronto: University of Toronto Press.
French, J. D. (1960), The reticular formation. In: *Handbook of Physiology,* Section 1: *Neurophysiology,* Vol. 2, ed. J. Field, H. W. Magoun, & V. Hall. Washington, DC: American Physiological Society, pp. 1281–1305.
Freud, A. (1937), The ego and the mechanisms of defense. In: *The Writings*

of Anna Freud, Vol. 2. New York: International Universities Press, 1966.
—— (1953), Some remarks on infant observation. *The Psychoanalytic Study of the Child,* 8:9–19. New York: International Universities Press.
—— (1960), Discussion of Dr. John Bowlby's paper. *The Psychoanalytic Study of the Child,* 15:53–62. New York: International Universities Press.
—— Burlingham, D. (1942), Part I: Monthly reports. In: *The Writings of Anna Freud,* 3:3–539. New York: International Universities Press, 1973.
—— —— (1944), Part II: Infants without families. In: *The Writings of Anna Freud,* 3:541–664. New York: International Universities Press, 1973.
—— Dann, S. (1951), An experiment in group upbringing. *The Psychoanalytic Study of the Child,* 6:127–168. New York: International Universities Press.
Freud, S. (1905), Three essays on the theory of sexuality. *Standard Edition,* 7:123–243. London: Hogarth Press, 1953.
—— (1911), Two principles of mental functioning. *Standard Edition,* 12:218–226. London: Hogarth Press, 1958.
—— (1913), Preface to Bourke's *Scatalogic Rites of All Nations. Standard Edition,* 12:333–337. London: Hogarth Press, 1958.
—— (1914), On narcissism: An introduction. *Standard Edition,* 14:67–102. London: Hogarth Press, 1957.
—— (1920), Beyond the pleasure principle. *Standard Edition,* 18:1–64. London: Hogarth Press, 1955.
—— (1921), Group psychology and the analysis of the ego. *Standard Edition,* 18:65–143. London: Hogarth Press, 1955.
—— (1926), Inhibitions, symptoms and anxiety. *Standard Edition,* 20:77–175. London: Hogarth Press, 1959.
Gardner, L. (1980), The endocrinology of abuse dwarfism. In: *Traumatic Abuse and Neglect of Children at Home,* ed. G. Williams & J. Money. Baltimore: Johns Hopkins University Press, pp. 375–380.
Garmezy, N., Masten, A., & Tellegen, A. (1984), The study of stress and competence in children. *Child Develop.,* 55:97–111.
Gindl, I., Hetzer, H., & Sturm, M. (1937), Unangemessenheit der Anstalt als Lebensraum für das Kleinkind: Zeitschrift Angewandte. *Psychol. Charakterkunde,* 52:310–358.
Goldfarb, W. (1943), Infant rearing and problem behavior. *Amer. J. Orthopsychiat.,* 13:249–265.
—— (1944), Infants' rearing as a factor in foster home replacement. *Amer. J. Orthopsychiat.,* 14:162–166.
Goleman, D. (1984), Some sexual behavior viewed as an addiction; Pattern of excessive sex is said to resemble alcoholism and compulsive gambling. *New York Times,* October 16, section C:1, 9.
Greenacre, P. (1945), The biological economy of birth. *The Psychoanalytic*

Study of the Child, 1:31-51. New York: International Universities Press.

——— (1953), Certain relationships between fetishism and faulty development of the body image. *The Psychoanalytic Study of the Child,* 8:79-98. New York: International Universities Press.

——— (1954), Problems of infantile neurosis: A discussion. *The Psychoanalytic Study of the Child,* 9:18-24. New York: International Universities Press.

——— (1959), Play in relation to creative imagination. *The Psychoanalytic Study of the Child,* 14:61-80. New York: International Universities Press.

Greenspan, S. (1979), *Intelligence and Adaptation: An Integration of Psychoanalytic and Piagetian Developmental Psychology.* New York: International Universities Press.

——— (1981), *Psychopathology and Adaptation in Infancy and Early Childhood.* New York: International Universities Press.

——— (1987), *Infants in Multirisk Families.* Madison, CT: International Universities Press.

——— (1989), *The Development of the Ego.* Madison, CT: International Universities Press.

——— (1992), *Infancy and Early Childhood.* Madison, CT: International Universities Press.

——— Lieberman, A. F. (1989), Infants, mothers and their interaction: A quantitative clinical approach to developmental assessment. In: *The Course of Life,* Vol. 1. Madison, CT: International Universities Press, pp. 503-560.

Harlow, H. F. (1958), The nature of love. *Amer. Psychol.,* 13:673-685.

——— (1962), The heterosexual affectional system in monkeys. *Amer. Psychol.,* 17:1-9.

——— Harlow, M. Q. (1962), Social deprivation in monkeys. *Scient. Amer.,* 207:137-146.

——— ——— Hansen, E. (1963), The maternal affectional system of rhesus monkeys. In: *Maternal Behavior in Mammals,* ed. H. Rheingold. New York: John Wiley, pp. 254-281.

Heath, R. (1964), Pleasure response of human subjects to direct stimulation of the brain. In: *The Role of Pleasure in Behavior,* ed. R. Heath. New York: Hoeber/Harper & Row, pp. 219-243.

——— Gallant, D. (1964), Activity of the human brain during emotional thought. In: *The Role of Pleasure in Behavior,* ed. R. Heath. New York: Hoeber/Harper & Row, pp. 87-96.

Hebb, D. O. (1958), The motivating effects of exteroceptive stimulation. *Amer. Psychol.,* 13:109-113.

Heron, W. (1961), Cognitive and physiological effects of perceptual isolation. In: *Sensory Deprivation,* ed. P. Solomon, P. Kubzansky, P. Leiderman, J. Mendelson, R. Trumbull, & D. Wexler. Cambridge, MA: Harvard University Press, pp. 6-33.

Hetzer, H., & Wolf, K. (1928), Baby tests. *Zeitschr. für Psychologie und Physiologie der Sinnesorgane,* 107:62–104.

Hilgard, E., & Marquis, D. (1940), *Conditioning and Learning,* rev. G. Kimble. New York: Appleton-Century-Crofts, 1961.

Hofer, M. (1983), On the relationship between attachment and separation processes in infancy. In: *Emotion, Theory, Research and Experience,* Vol. 2, ed. R. Plutchik & H. Kellerman. New York: Academic Press, pp. 199–219.

Hohman, L. B. (1922), Post-encephalitic behavior disorders in children. *Bull. Johns Hopkins,* 33:372–375.

Hollingworth, H. L. (1928), General laws of redintegration. *J. Gen. Psychol.,* 1:79–90.

Horney, K. (1937), *The Neurotic Personality of Our Time.* New York: W. W. Norton.

Hunt, J. McV. (1960), Experience and the development of motivation. *Child Develop.,* 31:489–504.

Jacobson, E. (1953), Metapsychology of cyclothymic depression. In: *Affective Disorders,* ed. P. Greenacre. New York: International Universities Press, pp. 49–83.

Jay, P. (1963), Mother–infant relations in Langurs. In: *Maternal Behavior in Mammals,* ed. H. Rheingold. New York: John Wiley, pp. 282–304.

Josselyn, I. (1956), Cultural forces, motherliness and fatherliness. *Amer. J. Orthopsychiat.,* 26:264–271.

Jung, C. G. (1921), Psychological types. In: *Collected Works,* Vol. 6. Princeton, NJ: Princeton University Press, 1971.

Kagan, J. (1980), *Infancy, Its Place in Human Development.* Cambridge, MA: Harvard University Press, pp. 175–259.

Karush, A. (1979), Introductory remarks on the role of empathy in the psychoanalytic process. *Bull. Assn. Psychoanal. Med.,* 18:62–63.

Kernberg, O. (1975), *Borderline Conditions and Pathological Narcissism.* New York: Jason Aronson.

Kestenberg, J., & Buelte, A. (1983), Prevention, infant therapy, and the treatment of adults, III. In: *Frontiers of Infant Psychiatry,* Vol. 1, ed. J. Call, E. Galenson, & R. Tyson. New York: Basic Books, pp. 200–216.

Khantzian, E. J., & Mack, J. E. (1983), Self preservation and the care of the self: Ego instincts reconsidered. *The Psychoanalytic Study of the Child,* 38:209–232. New Haven, CT: Yale University Press.

Kinsey, A., Martin, C., Pomeroy, W., & Gebhard, P. (1953), *Sexual Behavior in the Human Female.* Philadelphia: W. B. Saunders.

Klinnert, M., Campos, J., Sorce, J., Svejda, M., & Emde, R. (1983), Emotions as behavioral regulators. In: *Emotion, Theory, Research and Experience,* Vol. 2, ed. R. Plutchik & H. Kellerman. New York: Academic Press, pp. 57–86.

Koch, J. (1957), Change of excitability of the CNS in individual children during periods of wakefulness. *Cas Lek. Cesk.,* 96:757–765.

Kohen-Raz, R. (1968), Mental and motor development of kibbutz, institutionalized, and home-reared infants in Israel. *Child Develop.,* 39:489–504.

Kohut, H. (1977), *Restoration of the Self.* New York: International Universities Press.

—— (1984), *How Does Analysis Cure?* Chicago: University of Chicago Press.

Kolb, L. (1984). The post-traumatic stress disorders of combat: A subgroup with a conditioned emotional response. *Military Med.,* 149: 237–243.

Korner, A. (1964), Some hypotheses regarding the significance of individual differences at birth for later development. *The Psychoanalytic Study of the Child,* 19:58–72. New York: International Universities Press.

Kris, E. (1962), Decline and recovery in the life of a three-year-old. *The Psychoanalytic Study of the Child,* 17:175–215. New York: International Universities Press.

Lampl-de Groot, J. (1976), Mourning in a 6-year-old girl. *The Psychoanalytic Study of the Child,* 31:273–281. New York: International Universities Press.

Langmeier, J., & Matejcek, Z. (1975), *Psychological Deprivation in Childhood.* Queensland, Australia: University of Queensland Press.

Laplanche, J., & Pontalis, J. B. (1973), *The Language of Psychoanalysis.* New York: W. W. Norton.

Lewis, H. (1954), *Deprived Children: The Mersham Experiment.* New York: Oxford University Press.

Lewis, M., Mishkin, M., & Bragin, E. (1981), Opiate receptor gradients in the monkey cerebral cortex; correspondence with sensory processing hierarchies. *Science,* 211:1166–1169.

Lidz, T. (1975), *The Origin and Treatment of Schizophrenic Disorders.* Madison, CT: International Universities Press, 1990.

—— Lidz, R., & Rubenstein, R. (1976), An anaclitic syndrome in adolescent amphetamine addicts. *The Psychoanalytic Study of the Child,* 31:317–348. New Haven, CT: Yale University Press.

Lindsley, D. (1952), Psychological phenomena and the electroencephalogram. *Electroencephal. & Clin. Neurophysiol.,* 4:443–456.

Linnaeus (Carl Von Linné) (1758), *Systema Naturae,* 10th ed., Vol. 1. London: British Museum of Natural History, 1956.

Lipsitt, L. (1984), The pleasures and annoyances of babies. In: *Frontiers of Infant Psychiatry,* Vol. 2, ed. J. Call, E. Galenson, & R. Tyson. New York: Basic Books, pp. 82–94.

Luria, A. R. (1966), *Human Brain and Psychological Processes.* New York: Harper & Row.

—— Homskaya, E. D. (1964), Disturbance in the regulative role of speech with frontal lobe lesions. In: *The Frontal Granular Cortex and Behavior,* ed. J. M. Warren & K. Akert. New York: McGraw-Hill, pp. 353–371.

Magoun, H. (1958), Non-specific brain mechanisms. In: *Biological and Biochemical Bases of Behavior,* ed. H. Harlow & C. Woolsey. Madison: University of Wisconsin Press, pp. 25–36.

Mahler, M. (1968a), *On Human Symbiosis and the Vicissitudes of Individuation.* New York: International Universities Press.

—— (1968b), Adaptation and defense in statu nascendi. *Psychoanal. Quart.,* 37:1–21.

Maier, S., & Seligman, M. (1976), Learned helplessness, theory and evidence. *J. Experiment. Psychol. (General),* 105:3–46.

Main, M. (1990), Parental aversion to infant-initiated contact is correlated with the parent's own rejection during childhood. In: *Clinical Infant Reports: Touch,* ed. K. Barnard & T. B. Brazelton. Madison, CT: International Universities Press, pp. 461–495.

McCord, J. (1978), A thirty year follow-up of treatment effects. *Amer. Psychol.,* Vol. 33, No. 3, pp. 284–289.

Mittelmann, B. (1954), Motility in infants, children and adults: Patterning and psychodynamics. *The Psychoanalytic Study of the Child,* 9:142–177. New York: International Universities Press.

—— (1957), Motility in therapy of children and adults. *The Psychoanalytic Study of the Child,* 12:284–319. New York: International Universities Press.

Modell, A. (1990), *Other Times, Other Realities.* Cambridge, MA: Harvard University Press.

Moloney, J. C. (1949), *The Magic Cloak.* Wakefield, MA: Montrose Press.

Money, J. (1980), The syndrome of abuse dwarfism: Behavioral data and case report. In: *Traumatic Abuse and Neglect of Children at Home,* ed. G. Williams & J. Money. Baltimore: Johns Hopkins University Press, pp. 362–374.

—— Wolff, G. (1980), Late puberty, retarded growth and reversible hyposomatotropinism (psychosocial dwarfism). In: *Traumatic Abuse and Neglect of Children,* ed. G. Williams & J. Money. Baltimore: Johns Hopkins University Press, pp. 397–407.

Morrison, J., & Stewart, M. (1971), A family study of the hyperactive child syndrome. *Biolog. Psychiat.,* 3:189–195.

—— —— (1973), The psychiatric status of the legal families of adopted hyperactive children. *Arch. Gen. Psychiat.,* 28:888–891.

Moruzzi, G., & Magoun, H. (1949), Brain-stem reticular formation and activation of the E.E.G. In: *Electroencephal. & Clin. Neurophysiol.,* 1:455–473.

Mowrer, O. H. (1950), *Learning Theory and Personality Dynamics.* New York: Ronald Press.

Nachman, P., & Stern, D. (1984), Affect retrieval: A form of recall memory in prelinguistic infants. In: *Frontiers of Infant Psychaitry,* Vol. 2, ed. J. Call, E. Galenson, & R. Tyson. New York: Basic Books, pp. 95–100.

Newsweek, "New Theories About AIDS," January 30, 1984, pp. 50–52.

Olden, C. (1953), On adult empathy with children. *The Psychoanalytic Study of the Child,* 8:111–126. New York: International Universities Press.

Olds, J. (1958), Adaptive functions of paleocortical and related states. In: *Biological and Biochemical Bases of Behavior,* ed. H. Harlow & C. Woolsey. Madison: University of Wisconsin Press, pp. 237–262.

—— (1964), The mechanisms of voluntary behavior. In: *The Role of Pleasure in Behavior,* ed. R. Heath. New York: Hoeber/Harper & Row, pp. 23–53.

Orford, J. (1985), *Excessive Appetites: A Psychological View of Addictions.* New York: John Wiley.

Panksepp, J. (1980), Brief social isolation, pain responsivity and morphine analgesia in young rats. *Psychopharmacol.,* 72:111–112.

Pfaundler, M. (1925), Klinik und Fürsorge. *Gesundheitsfürsorge Kindesalter,* 1:3–17.

Pribram, K. (1960), The intrinsic systems of the forebrain. In: *Handbook of Physiology,* Section 1: *Neurophysiology,* Vol. 2, ed. J. Field, H. W. Magoun, & V. Hall. Washington, DC: American Physiological Society, pp. 1323–1344.

Provence, S. (1983), Struggling against deprivation and trauma: A longitudinal case study. *The Psychoanalytic Study of the Child,* 38:233–256. New Haven, CT: Yale University Press.

—— Lipton, R. (1962), *Infants in Institutions.* New York: International Universities Press.

Prugh, D. G., & Harlow, R. (1966), Masked deprivation in infants and young children. In: *Deprivation of Maternal Care, A Reassessment of Its Effects,* presented in conjunction with John Bowlby's *Maternal Care and Mental Health.* New York: Schocken Books, pp. 201–221.

Quadland, M. (1987), AIDS, sexuality, and sexual control. *J. Homosexual.,* 14:277–298.

Reich, A. (1936), A clinical contribution to the understanding of the paranoid personality. In: *Annie Reich: Psychoanalytic Contributions.* New York: International Universities Press, 1973, pp. 46–84.

—— (1960), Pathological forms of self-esteem regulation. *The Psychoanalytic Study of the Child,* 15:215–232. New York: International Universities Press.

Ribble, M. (1965), *The Rights of Infants.* New York: Columbia University Press.

Ritchie, J. M. (1985), The aliphatic alcohols. In: *The Pharmacological Basis of Therapeutics,* 7th ed., ed. A. Gilman, L. Goodman, T. Rall, & F. Murad. New York: Macmillan, pp. 372–386.

Robertson, J. (1962), Mothering as an influence on early development: A study of well-baby clinic records. *The Psychoanalytic Study of the Child,* 17:245–264. New York: International Universities Press.

—— Robertson, J. (1971–1972), Young children in brief separation. *The Psychoanalytic Study of the Child,* 26:264–315. New York: International Universities Press.

Rochlin, G. (1953), Loss and restitution. *The Psychoanalytic Study of the Child,* 8:288–309. New York: International Universities Press.
—— (1965), *Griefs and Discontents.* Boston: Little, Brown.
Rosen, J. (1968), *Selected Papers on Direct Analysis,* Vol. 2. New York: Grune & Stratton.
Rubenfine, D. (1962), Maternal stimulation, psychic structure, and early object relations. *The Psychoanalytic Study of the Child,* 17:265–282. New York: International Universities Press.
Rutter, M. (1971), Parent–child separation. *J. Child Psychol. & Psychiat.,* 12:233–260.
—— (1979), Maternal deprivation 1972–1978: New findings, new concepts, new approaches. *Child Develop.,* 50:283–305.
—— (1987), Psychosocial resilience and protective mechanisms. *Amer. J. Orthopsychiat.,* 57:316–331.
Sander, L. (1975), Infant and caretaking environment. In: *Explorations in Child Psychiatry,* ed. E. J. Anthony. New York: Plenum Press, pp. 129–166.
—— (1983), Polarity, paradox, and the organizing process in development. In: *Frontiers in Infant Psychiatry,* Vol. 1, ed. J. Call, E. Galenson, & R. Tyson. New York: Basic Books, pp. 333–346.
Schafer, R. (1954), *Psychoanalytic Interpretation in Rorschach Testing.* New York: Grune & Stratton.
—— (1959), Generative empathy in the treatment situation. *Psychoanal. Quart.,* 28:342–373.
Schlossmann, A. (1920), Zur Frage der Säuglingssterblichkeit in Anstalten. *Müenchener Medizinische Wochenschrift,* 67:1318–1320.
—— (1923), Die Entwicklung der Versorgung kranker Säuglinge in Anstalten. *Ergebnisse Inneren Medizin Kinderheilkunde,* 24:188–209.
Schorer, M. (1961), *Sinclair Lewis.* New York: McGraw-Hill.
Seligman, M., & Peterson, C. (1986), A learned helplessness perspective on childhood depression. In: *Depression in Young People,* ed. M. Rutter, C. Izard, & P. Read. New York: Guilford Press, pp. 223–249.
Selye, H. (1976), *Stress in Health and Disease.* London: Butterworth.
Severy, L., & Whitaker, M. (1982), Juvenile diversion: An experimental analysis of effectiveness of treatment. *Eval. Rev.,* 6:759–772.
Spiegel, N. (1967), An infantile fetish and its persistence into young womanhood. *The Psychoanalytic Study of the Child,* 22:402–425. New York: International Universities Press.
Spitz, R. (1945), Hospitalism: An inquiry into the genesis of psychiatric conditions in early childhood. *The Psychoanalytic Study of the Child,* 1:53–74. New York: International Universities Press.
—— (1946), Hospitalism: A follow-up report. *The Psychoanalytic Study of the Child,* 2:113–117. New York: International Universities Press.
—— (1951), The psychogenic diseases in infancy. *The Psychoanalytic Study of the Child,* 6:255–275. New York: International Universities Press.

—— Wolf, K. M. (1946), Anaclitic depression. *The Psychoanalytic Study of the Child*, 2:313–342. New York: International Universities Press.

Sroufe, L. A. (1989), Relationships, self, and individual adaptation. In: *Relationship Disturbances in Early Childhood*, ed. A. J. Sameroff & R. N. Emde. New York: Basic Books, pp. 70–94.

Steele, B. (1980), Psychodynamic factors in child abuse. In: *The Battered Child*, ed. C. H. Kempe & R. Helfer. Chicago: University of Chicago Press, pp. 49–85.

—— (1983), The effect of abuse and neglect on psychological development. In: *Frontiers of Infant Psychiatry*, Vol. 1, ed. J. Call, E. Galenson, & R. Tyson. New York: Basic Books, pp. 235–244.

—— (1986), Lasting effects of early child abuse. In: *Child Abuse & Neglect, Internat. J.,* 10:283–291.

Stern, D. (1974), The goal and structure of mother–infant play. *J. Amer. Acad. Child Psychiat.,* 13:402–421.

—— (1983), Early transmission of affect. In: *Frontiers of Infant Psychiatry*, Vol. 1, ed. J. Call, E. Galenson, & R. Tyson. New York: Basic Books, pp. 74–84.

Stone, E., Bonnet, K., & Hofer, M. A. (1976), Survival and development of maternally deprived rats: Role of body temperature. *Psychosom. Med.,* 38:242–249.

Straus, B. (1980), *Maladies of Marcel Proust.* New York: Holmes & Meier.

Sullivan, H. S. (1953), *The Interpersonal Theory of Psychiatry.* New York: W. W. Norton.

Suomi, S. J. (1990), The role of tactile contact in rhesus monkey social development. In: *Touch*, ed. K. E. Barnard & T. B. Brazelton. Madison, CT: International Universities Press, pp. 129–164.

Teitelbaum, P. (1967), The biology of drive. In: *The Neurosciences*, ed. G. C. Quarton, T. Melnechuk, & F. O. Schmitt. New York: Rockefeller University Press, pp. 557–567.

Thomas, A., & Chess, S. (1977), *Temperament and Development.* New York: Brunner/Mazel.

—— —— (1980), *The Dynamics of Psychological Development.* New York: Brunner/Mazel.

Tizard, B., Cooperman, O., Joseph, A., & Tizard, J. (1972), Environmental effects on language development: A study of young children in long-stay residential nurseries. *Child Develop.,* 43:337–358.

Vaillant, G. (1983), *The Natural History of Alcoholism.* Cambridge, MA: Harvard University Press.

van der Kolk, B. (1987), *Psychological Trauma.* Washington, DC: American Psychiatric Press.

—— Boyd, H., Krystal, J., & Greenberg, M. (1984), Post-traumatic stress disorder: Implications of the animal model of inescapable shock. In: *Post-Traumatic Stress Disorders, Psychological and Biological Sequellae*, ed. B. van der Kolk. Washington, DC: American Psychiatric Press, pp. 125–126.

Velasquez, J., & Lyle, C. (1985), Day versus residential treatment for juvenile offenders. *Child Welfare,* 64:145–156.

Ward, A. (1957), Efferent functions of the reticular formation. In: *Reticular Formation of the Brain,* ed. H. Jasper, L. Proctor, R. Knighton, W. Noshay, & R. Costello. Boston: Little, Brown, pp. 263–273.

Weil, J. (1989a), *Instinctual Stimulation of Children,* Vol. 1. Madison, CT: International Universities Press.

—— (1989b), *Instinctual Stimulation of Children,* Vol. 2. Madison, CT: International Universities Press.

—— (unpublished), Case of Louis, a withdrawn boy seen in therapy from the age of ten through twenty-five years.

—— (unpublished), Case of Paul, age seven to ten years, an intelligent but compulsive boy with severe learning problems.

Werner, H. (1957), The concept of development from a comparative and organismic point of view. In: *The Concept of Development,* ed. D. B. Harris. Minneapolis: University of Minnesota Press, pp. 125–148.

White, R. (1963), Ego and Reality in Psychoanalytic Theory. *Psychological Issues,* Monograph 11, Vol. 3, No. 3. New York: International Universities Press.

Winnicott, D. W. (1960a), The theory of the parent–infant relationship. In: *The Maturational Processes and the Facilitating Environment.* New York: International Universities Press, 1965, pp. 37–55.

—— (1960b), Ego distortion in terms of true and false self. In: *The Maturational Processes and the Facilitating Environment.* New York: International Universities Press, 1965, pp. 140–152.

—— (1963a), Casework and mental illness. In: *The Maturational Processes and the Facilitating Environment.* New York: International Universities Press, 1965, pp. 217–229.

—— (1963b), Psychiatric disorder in terms of infantile maturational processes. In: *The Maturational Processes and the Facilitating Environment.* New York: International Universities Press, 1965, pp. 230–241.

—— (1963c), Dependence in infant-care, in child-care, and in the psychoanalytic setting. In: *The Maturational Processes and the Facilitating Environment.* New York: International Universities Press, 1965, pp. 249–259.

Wolff, P. (1960), The Developmental Psychologies of Jean Piaget and Psychoanalysis. *Psychological Issues,* Monogr. 5, Vol. 2, No. 1. New York: International Universities Press.

—— (1966), The Causes, Control and Organization of Behavior in the Neonate. *Psychological Issues,* Monogr. 17, Vol. 5, No. 1. New York: International Universities Press.

—— (1987), *Behavioral States and the Expression of Emotions in Early Infancy.* Chicago: University of Chicago Press.

Wolfenstein, M. (1955), Mad laughter in a six-year old boy. *The Psy-*

choanalytic Study of the Child, 10:381–394. New York: International Universities Press.

Yorke, C., & Wiseberg, S. (1976), A developmental view of anxiety: Some clinical and theoretical considerations. *The Psychoanalytic Study of the Child,* 31:107–135. New Haven, CT: Yale University Press.

Zavitzianos, G. (1990), Homosexuality and homovestism: Developmental aspects. In: *The Homosexualities,* ed. C. W. Socarides & V. D. Volkan. Madison, CT: International Universities Press.

Zingg, R. M. (1940), Feral man and extreme cases of isolation. *Amer. J. Psychol.,* 53:487–517.

Zuckerman, M. (1979), *Sensation Seeking.* Hillsdale, NJ: Lawrence Erlbaum.

AUTHOR INDEX

SUBJECT INDEX